John Irving

Twayne's United States Authors Series

Warren French, Editor

Indiana University

TUSAS 502

John Irving

By Carol C. Harter
and James R. Thompson

Ohio University

Twayne Publishers • Boston

John Irving

Carol C. Harter
James R. Thompson

Copyright © 1986 by G. K. Hall & Co.
All Rights Reserved
Published by Twayne Publishers
A Division of G. K. Hall & Co.
70 Lincoln Street
Boston, Massachusetts 02111

Frontispiece reproduced by permission
of Mary Ellen Mark/Archive

Copyediting supervised by Lewis De Simone
Book production by Elizabeth Todesco
Book design by Barbara Anderson

Typeset in 11 pt. Garamond
by P&M Typesetting, Inc., Waterbury, Connecticut

Printed on permanent/durable acid-free paper
and bound in the United States of America

Library of Congress Cataloging in Publication Data

Harter, Carol C.
   John Irving.

   (Twayne's United States authors series; TUSAS 502)
   Bibliography: p. 154
   Includes index.
   1. Irving, John, 1942–   —Criticism and
interpretation. I. Thompson, James R.   II. Title.
III. Series.
PS3559.R8Z68   1986   813'.54   85-30533
ISBN 0-8057-7462-9

For Michael Harter and Janice Thompson

Contents

About the Authors

Carol C. Harter is an associate professor of English and American literature and vice president for administration at Ohio University, Athens, Ohio. She received the B.A. with honors from Harpur College and the M.A. and Ph.D. from the State University of New York at Binghamton with a "distinguished" dissertation on Faulkner.

In addition to performing administrative duties and writing about managerial issues, Dr. Harter continues to teach and write on American literary topics. She has published articles on various American figures, including Emerson, Dreiser, Eliot, Faulkner, Joyce Carol Oates, and several Ohio-based writers, and is particularly interested in contemporary American novelists.

James R. Thompson is a professor of English and American literature at Ohio University, Athens, Ohio. He received the B.A. and M.A. degrees from Bowling Green State University and the Ph.D. degree from the University of Cincinnati, where he was a Howard Taft Fellow.

Professor Thompson has written and lectured on the English Romantic poets and on American fiction, and he has been a Fulbright lecturer on American literature at the University of Graz, Austria. He has previously contributed *Leigh Hunt* and *Thomas Lovell Beddoes* to Twayne's English Authors Series.

At present Carol Harter and James Thompson are cowriting a book on the novelist E. L. Doctorow.

Preface

John Irving has now published six novels in seventeen years. Relatively obscure until 1978 when his *The World According to Garp* emerged as one of the major literary successes of the decade, Irving has since had two more novels on the best-seller list. His unique mix of subject matter and style, his close identification with the so-called "Garp phenomenon," and the wide popularity of his novels have made him something of a minor culture hero.

Enormous popularity and financial success have not, however, earned him unequivocal critical praise. Scholarly articles, doctoral dissertations, and one book-length study have appeared, but response to Irving's work includes not only serious analysis and respect but, at the other extreme, contemptuous dismissal.

Irving, who has referred to his fictional materials as having "all the ingredients of an X-rated soap opera,"[1] writes to and about a majority readership; his inspiration is Dickens, his dread the Barths, Coovers, Pynchons, and the host of scavenging academics in their wake. His use of popular materials and his desire for a very large audience outrage some critics. William H. Pritchard, for example—"as a guardian of minority culture against mass civilization and novelists who allow themselves to exploit it"[2]—loathed *Garp* so much that he found it impossible to approach Irving's next novel with anything even approaching objectivity. To Pritchard the question of Irving is part of a cultural battle, a battle he is confident Irving will lose.

Irving has brought his comic-tragic vision to bear on the materials of mass culture, but his performance and comments both suggest motives more complex than Pritchard and other Irving detractors would admit. With mixed degrees of success, he has attempted to mediate between "high" art and mass culture because, unlike some of his contemporaries, he still believes in the value of the novel as a popular form—in the ability of the writer to delight *and* instruct. In an age in which many of this country's most impressive talents have chosen (or been forced) to view the novel as little more than an intellectual and creative game, Irving appears to take it—and its audience—seriously.

The secondary theme in the following short but comprehensive study of Irving's work is this curious fusion of literary idealism, aesthetic concerns, and mass materials. After an introduction to the man and his work, subsequent chapters will examine each of his novels as they emerge, focusing on the individual texts but also observing the inter-relatedness of Irving's materials as well as his artistic development.

Carol C. Harter
James R. Thompson

Ohio University

Acknowledgments

We are grateful to Random House for permission to quote from *Setting Free the Bears, The Water-Method Man* and *The 158-Pound Marriage;* to E. P. Dutton for permission to quote from *The World According to Garp* and *The Hotel New Hampshire;* and to William Morrow for permission to quote from *The Cider House Rules.* We also wish to thank Mary Ellen Mark/Archive for permission to use the fine photograph of John Irving and his sons, and to recognize the formidable secretarial skills and endless patience of Roseann Sedwick and Carol Blue. Finally, it is with great pleasure that we acknowledge the personal kindness and essential editorial leadership of Dr. Warren French.

Chronology

1942   John Winslow Irving born at Exeter, New Hampshire.

1961   Graduates, Phillips Exeter Academy.

1961–1962   University of Pittsburgh.

1963–1964   Institute of European Studies, University of Vienna.

1964   Marries Shyla Leary.

1965   Graduates cum laude, University of New Hampshire; son Colin born.

1967   M.F.A., University of Iowa.

1968   *Setting Free the Bears.*

1969–1971   Resides in Putney, Vermont and Vienna.

1970   Son Brendan born.

1972   Rockefeller Foundation grant; *The Water-Method Man.*

1972–1975   Writer-in-residence, Writer's Workshop, University of Iowa.

1974   *The 158-Pound Marriage.*

1974–1975   NEA Fellowship.

1975–1978   Assistant professor of English, Mount Holyoke College.

1976–1977   Guggenheim Foundation grant.

1978   *The World According to Garp.*

1980   *Garp* awarded American Book Award as best paperback novel of 1979.

1981   *The Hotel New Hampshire.*

1985   *The Cider House Rules.*

Chapter One
The Man and the Writer: "Novelist as Cultural Hero"

On the eve of the 1981 publication of John Irving's fifth novel, *The Hotel New Hampshire,*[1] *Time* magazine (in its 31 August cover story) described the novelist as the "most successful 'serious' young writer in America." Linking him with Salinger and Vonnegut, the critic confidently assured us that "the end of the [last] decade belonged to Irving." The huge sales of Irving's immensely popular *The World According to Garp,* the writer's "dark, heartthrob good looks," his runner-wrestler's physique ("not since Hemingway has a well-known American writer worked as hard on his body as he has on his prose") all encouraged *Time's* R. Z. Sheppard to exult over "Garpomania," with its six color choice paperbacks and T-shirts sporting Garpian slogans.[2]

The article in *Time* magazine—one of the house organs of popular culture—naturally helped to promote as well as to document the personality cult that had already come to surround Irving, but Sheppard had not created it. Irving, who has become sensitive to observations concerning the tensions between fame and financial success on one side and critical approval on the other, had earlier carried vanity plates on his car hyping two of his novels and if he eventually came to resent the willingness of others to make judgments about his life and art, he had clearly cooperated with image makers and encouraged that status. The aloof artist who can casually refer to a reviewer as his "inferior in every way"[3] has nonetheless lent himself to muscular advertisements for dictionaries, provided beefcake portraits for *Vanity Fair,* and opened his Park Avenue kitchen to an interviewer from *Mademoiselle* who pertly asked him how his new role—"the novelist as cultural hero, as sex symbol"—had affected his life. Irving's response on that occasion was a mixture of cliché and ingenuousness: "except [for] the luxury to write full-time" (presumably when not helping to make movies or entertaining the mass media), his huge "success has changed very little" for him. "My fame is really the least interesting thing about me" he claimed, and implied that his extraliterary visibility merely offered him a way of getting even with "detractors"—"it's nice to make other people angrier than they make you." Besides, as a writer who had "worked in obscurity for years," he always remembers having promised himself that he "would never become grateful" when fame did arrive.[4] Nor does he appear to have forgotten; there is, in these statements, the tone of lines rehearsed.

In *Vogue* magazine, in the post-*Garp* days, Irving appeared quite willing to write a piece called "Best Seller: What Does It Really Mean." There in a single column he disposes of current American film, theater, and painting (while in the later *Mademoiselle* interview he speaks with contempt of a reviewer's willingness to dispose of a single novel in "twenty-five hundred words or less").[5] Quoting Solzhenitsyn on the increasingly trivial nature of a culture defined solely by the mass media, Irving concludes the *Vogue* piece with the reasonable axiom "good reading is the country's salvation,"[6] thus taking his place as a sort of pop-culture Matthew Arnold.

In more serious ways, too, Irving as man and writer has been identified with the current issues and interests of American life. In 1982, for example, *Ms.* magazine voted him one of its twenty-five "heroes" for "integrating feminism as a major philosophical theme,"[7] the only writer on a list that includes such high visibility figures as television's Phil Donahue, the actor Alan Alda, and Admiral Elmo Zumwalt. Only a month later the same magazine featured an article on "The 'Garp' Phenomenon" by novelist Marilyn French (herself no stranger to popular fiction) in which both Irving's novel and the film based on it are taken to task for offering a "frenzy of obscene violence" which appears to demonstrate the author's belief "that feminism is a violent response to male sexuality."[8] Her conclusion that his analysis of a "major philosophical theme" has failed, or worse, that Irving has simply exploited certain sensational aspects of contemporary life, demands a vigorous repudiation—neither Irving's fiction nor its relationship to society is that simple—but that he has always closely tuned his ear to our cultural songs seems clear, as a glance back at his subjects will attest. After two novels vaguely cognizant of the counterculture then ascendant, Irving's next three works are, at least superficially, described by his own observation that *Garp* "has all the ingredients of an X-rated soap opera"[9]: a "wife-swapping" novel is succeeded by a feminism-and-violence book and that is followed by a novel that extends those themes and adds terrorism. Irving's latest novel, *The Cider House Rules,* graphically dramatizes the abortion controversy in America and is, he claims, "a book with a polemic."[10] Irving himself and the novelist hero of *Garp* have discussed and defended the use of such materials by the serious artist, and the issue will be discussed in this study as well.

What appears to have the greatest symbolic significance for Sheppard in his *Time* cover story, however, is not so much the subject matter or value of Irving's fiction as it is the filming of *Garp* then underway by director George Roy Hill. Years earlier Irving had worked with filmmaker Irvin Kershner on an abortive screenplay of his first novel, *Setting Free the Bears.* Now Irving was not only coaching the film's lead in wrestling; he was himself to appear briefly in the movie as a referee. Irving's status as American popular culture hero had thus been consecrated when a big movie was made from a big book and its author could actually be *seen* on the big screen; needless to say, that consecration was to be validated by *Time's* own story. It should not then be surprising (if nevertheless disconcerting) that the paperback book jacket of *Garp* describes Irving as having "been a bartender, wrestling coach, movie star, and college professor, as well as writer."[11]

Writer in Residence

Only after reporting on the stuff of casual fame does *Time* mention Irving's then current stint at the Bread Loaf Writer's Conference, a gathering he had attended before, along with such important names (though not ablaze in the mass media) as Stanley Elkin and the late John Gardner. Yet that footnote is of special significance, since it points to an essential and particularly American paradox in Irving's career; the well-established personality, the enormously successful commercial writer of *Garp* had had, for all his occasional satire of the academy, a nearly paradigmatic career as a university writer—Bread Loaf being almost exactly where you would expect him to be on a fine August afternoon in 1981.

John Winslow Irving was raised in the academic establishment. Born in Exeter, New Hampsire, on 1 March 1942, his stepfather was a teacher of Russian history at the town's prestigious Phillips Exeter Academy and Irving was educated there, graduating in 1961 after a career distinguished more by his enthusiasm for wrestling and writing than for general academic achievement.[12] Reared in a world of excellent educational possibility, he was to remain, for the most part, inside academia until 1978 when, freed by the success of *Garp* from the teaching he did not especially enjoy, he was able to devote himself to the writing he loved. The years between Exeter and *Garp* are filled with the typical experiences and conditions of a great many American writers: degrees, teaching positions, foreign travel, and fellowships. In 1963–1964, after Exeter (and a fruitless year at the University of Pittsburgh where he had been lured by the chance to wrestle), Irving attended the University of Vienna's Institute in European Studies, a place chosen for its exotic atmosphere rather than its school, an environment in which he could find the necessary "sense of anonymity" and learn how to "pay attention" passionately.[13] Austria thereby became, whether as simple location or complex symbol, central to each of his first five novels. In August 1964 he was married to Shyla Leary, a photographer and former Radcliffe student he had met at Cambridge before departing for Europe.

By the fall of 1964 the young couple was back in New England, Irving to re-enroll in the University of New Hampshire (where he had earlier studied briefly) and Shyla to give birth to their first son, Colin, in 1965. Also in that year Irving received his B.A. degree cum laude.

In Austria Irving had begun and abandoned a mad rodeo novel set in New England and at New Hampshire he wrote a least two publishable stories, "A Winter Branch," which appeared in *Redbook* in 1965, and "Weary Kingdom," published three years later in the *Boston Review*. Both stories have the air of creative writing classes about them and it is not surprising, therefore, that after graduating he moved his family west where he enrolled in the University of Iowa's long-established Writers' Workshop. At New Hampshire he had worked under two academic novelists (Thomas Williams, *The Hair of Harold Roux*, and John Yount, *Wolf at the Door*); at Iowa he would study with Vance Bourjaily and Kurt Vonnegut, the latter of whom would read his first novel, *Setting Free the Bears*, before it appeared in 1968, the year after Irving received his M.F.A. from Iowa.

For many serious American writers the university remains essential to their temporary and sometimes permanent economic survival, while at the same time producing a continuous drain on their energy and limitations on their time. And while they move in a circle of their colleagues' and students' admiration, they must devote much of their attention to the work of *other* minds. In such circumstances frustration and ambivalence are to be expected. For the next ten years Irving was to hold various posts in such a world: first at the now defunct Windham College in Putney, Vermont, and then (after another stay in Vienna, this time to write and to work on a screenplay of *Bears*) at Iowa's Writers' Workshop (1972–1975) and Mount Holyoke College (1975–1978).

Also characteristic of the university writer's career were the grants (a source of freedom to write but also a recognition of success inside the academy): a Rockefeller Foundation grant in 1972, a National Endowment for the Arts fellowship in 1974–75, and a Guggenheim in 1976–77. But Irving was a serious writer and in 1972, Random House, publisher of *Bears,* published his excellent second novel, *The Water-Method Man,* and two years later *The 158-Pound Marriage.* A difference of opinion concerning the cause of low sales, despite good reviews, of those novels motivated Irving, with Random House's concurrence, to move to E. P. Dutton; there the late Henry Robbins, skilled editor of Joan Didion and Stanley Elkin, convinced the firm that *Garp* was "sure to be the 'breakthrough' book by an immensely talented novelist."[14] The novel's publication in 1978 added enormous financial success to an already growing critical reputation; whereas *The Water-Method Man,* at slightly fewer than 7,000 copies, had been till then his best-selling novel, *Garp* sold more than 100,000 hardcover copies before the over three million paperbacks that were to follow. It earned Irving, moreover, the National Book Award for the best paperback novel of 1979.

By 1978 Irving was living back in Putney, Vermont, where he remained until moving to the Park Avenue apartment in which he presently resides. In 1981 Dutton brought out another big novel, *The Hotel New Hampshire.* Shortly after its publication, he separated from his wife Shyla. Following his fifth book Irving had suggested that his next novel would be a small, Turgenev-like work.[15] In the spring of 1985, however, William Morrow, his third publisher, released the large, almost Dickensian novel, *The Cider House Rules.*

Popular Culture and Serious Art

Juxtaposing Irving's role as mass entertainer against his long association with the university reminds us of the endlessly replicated and critical American paradox: from the outset we have been a nation of materialists and idealists, doers and knowers. Literary success is inevitably caught up in this paradox; expectations, depending upon the vantage point, range from commercial to aesthetic and these seemingly exclusive demands produce enormous tensions—often constructive but sometimes, as in the case of F. Scott Fitzgerald, destructive. Writers must always be aware of their implications; even should they sincerely discount significant material reward they must still recognize that access to readers is itself contingent on some degree of popular success. But beyond this basic reality lies the fact that, shaped by the forces and values of our society, material success must play some role in one's sense of self-worth; the artist is hardly immune to the conditioning process of the reward system. "We destroy them in many ways," Hemingway argued in *Green Hills of Africa,* speaking of the pressures brought to bear on American novelists, "first economically. They make money . . . increase their standard of living and . . . are caught."[16]

This discussion is not meant to suggest that Irving suffers a cultural schizophrenia, but rather to call attention to the way in which he has chosen to mediate between popular culture and "serious" art. He is rightly suspicious that some of the adverse criticism he has received results from the academy's perhaps unconscious assumption that excellence and poverty equate, that good writing cannot possibly produce a wide following. He was understandably amazed to find that an old friend, upon returning to America after a long absence, was shocked and apparently upset to learn that *Garp* had enjoyed more than twenty weeks on the best-seller list. "I suppose you're happy about this," the friend commented, "but how do you like the company you're keeping?"[17] Irving's motive in citing his friend's distaste is not to defend best sellers—most "are terrible books, many . . . not even readable books"—but rather to justify his own choice. Books, he argues, "are the only medium where the insistence of a deliberate and personal vision stands even half a chance to reach a wide audience." Unlike filmmakers, for instance, writers in their solitary craft can be "wise in the way only personal, unique visions can be wise."[18] Irving's argument remains valid, despite the obvious contradiction—or at least tension—between the demands of "personal vision" and "wide audience."

The belief Irving expresses here (as well as even the language used to express it) is fully consonant with older humanistic assumptions of the academy. Though often guilty of a perversely myopic focus, the traditional academic teacher-critic nevertheless believes in the humanistic values inherent in the free exercise of the verbal imagination and, contemplating the world from a position not wholly subordinated to a market economy, has the luxury of emphasizing those high aesthetic standards established by the example of great writers of the past. Despite all the fashionable academic debate over postmodernism and deconstruction, such a figure would no doubt warmly agree with Irving that "good reading is this country's salvation."

The novels of John Irving, especially *The World According to Garp, The Hotel New Hampshire,* and *The Cider House Rules,* clearly reflect his acute awareness of, and sympathy with, the elements of popular literature and the world that literature reflects. Despite eccentricities (for example, his connection with Austria), his preoccupation is with the serious and ludicrous elements of modern American society, not seen simply from the perspective of a realist or a modernist-absurdist, but from the perspective of one sensitive to the legitimacy of those elements as sympathetic literary material. The focus of popular fiction is his focus. In exploring these areas—marriage, murder, love, rape, terrorism, abortion—he authenticates them while transcending the limits of their treatment by those writers who would exploit them merely for easy commercial success.

This attitude is reflected in the literary theory articulated in his novels, in the narrative design of the last three, and in many of his statements about fiction:

> Art has an *aesthetic* responsibility to be entertaining. The writer's responsibility is to take hard stuff and make it as accessible as the stuff can be made. Art and entertainment aren't contradictions. It's only been in the last decade, or twenty years, that there has somehow developed this rubric under which art is *expected* to be difficult. Why? On the basis of some sort of self-congratulation of the strenuousness required of us? This notion seems to me to be, frankly, a way of perpetuating the middleman, the academic who might be necessary to explain the difficult work for us. By creating a taste for literature that needs interpretation, we, of course, create jobs for reviewers, for critics, for the academy. I like books that can be read without those middlemen.[19]

That Irving invents enemies and dangers here (the Barths and the Pynchons and their explicators have never really threatened to dominate the novel's audience or destroy it as a form) and that he oversimplifies and foreshortens literary history and criticism (the examples of such complex geniuses as Joyce and Faulkner come immediately to mind) is not the real issue. Rather, it is his hatred of "elitism" (the "preciousness, the specialness of so much contemporary fiction") which he *believes* threatens to transform the novel, "once the most public of forms," into the solipsistic and obscure genre he finds contemporary poetry to be.[20]

He therefore requires, and, as we have seen, has overwhelmingly attained, a truly wide audience. He continually emphasizes narrative—the basis for any popular fiction—and he again and again creates characters who emerge from and speak for that very audience itself. That fact is nowhere more evident than in the character of Jillsy Sloper in *The World According to Garp*. Indeed, in Jillsy, Irving creates an "everyreader"—an articulate, insightful, and commonsensical lover of Garp's work whose advice the artist-character both seeks and accepts. Moreover, he believes in the advice despite the fact that he has struggled throughout the novel with the frustrating realization that his mother Jenny's book is wildly popular and yet virtually without artistic merit.

But the novels illustrate an impulse to create work of sophisticated symbolic and metaphoric value while *simultaneously* appealing to an audience on whom "high art" would be lost; this goal becomes a personal commitment of Irving the artist, as well as a discrete theme in his novels. The popularity of Irving's fiction with a wide audience is demonstrated at every bookstand. Critical and scholarly analysis has, however, been mixed, and discussion among academics indicates that the status of Irving's work as serious literature remains controversial. Since his popular success can be documented, the issue must then be how effectively Irving creates art demanding careful study, analysis, and formal explication—whatever his stated intentions. Does it embody and shape significant human experience in sophisticated symbolic constructs? Does the emotive experience of his work have the power to create the shock of insight into human values the way "high art" by definition does?

These questions must be answered positively. His best fiction is embodied in artistically successful forms that will support serious analysis. Equally important, Irving's interest in the popular audience—in the woman from Findlay, Ohio, whom Garp struggles vainly to convince of his humanistic motives as a writer—is in a modern sense Arnoldian: he respects but would educate its humanity, not simply exploit its taste. Meeting her world on its own ground he seeks to enlarge, through his own comic-tragic vision, its self-aware-

ness and capacity for sympathy. Hence, however eccentric his characters may appear, they are never actually exotic, nor are their lives
embodiments of some complex and arcane psychological or social theory. Rather, they offer us patterns of reality heightened by a sense of
their significance and seen, as he argues they must be, through the
lens of a personal vision.

Tradition and Innovation

A discussion of the relationship between popular and "high art" in
Irving's fiction leads one naturally to the issue of Irving's experiments
with form and technique. And while some might question the description of Irving as an experimental writer, it is nonetheless true
that he self-consciously employs traditional forms, *not* in recognizable
and predictable patterns overtly designed to create the familiar and
comfortable experience of popular fiction. Rather, in much of his
fiction Irving seems to experiment with the limits of traditional forms
in an attempt to discover how malleable and adaptable they are to a
thoroughly modern vision of experience.

Likewise, Irving reinvigorates the third-person narrative perspective. Rather than seduce us into the solipsistic view of the modern
protagonist whose subjective vision defines the parameters in which
the fiction's world must be experienced, Irving blends subjective *and*
objective perspectives, either by creating two equally important
figures—one of whom observes and one of whom acts (for example,
Severin Winter and the narrator in *The 158-Pound Marriage,* and John
and Franny Berry in *The Hotel New Hampshire*)—or by creating an "I"
narrative within a quasibiographical frame, a technique he uses in a
somewhat unsophisticated way in his first novel, *Setting Free the Bears,*
and perfects in *The World According to Garp.* In his latest novel, *The
Cider House Rules,* Irving has employed a modified version of the
Dickensian omniscient narrator.

Indeed, the refraction of perspective in *Garp* is multidimensional.
The voice in the narrative frame begins the story before Garp's birth
and ends with an epilogue which clearly extends beyond his death by
many years. This technique, used extensively in eighteenth and nineteenth-century fiction, is itself an interesting anachronism and is designed at least partially to create objective distance, to provide an
external analysis and judgment of Garp's experience.

This narrative voice, however, is blended with a direct access to Garp's intellectual, emotional, and artistic perspective as the narrator quotes his observations, reveals his letters verbatim, and integrates his stories directly into the narrative fabric. This layering effect serves simultaneously to embody the intimate and personal, while providing the objective, filtering, and balancing point of view of the disinterested observer.

Novels, Irving has claimed, are "what people wish would be their lives."[21] From another perspective they are also to him what their lives should be. Nowhere is the duality of Irving's use of tradition and innovation more evident than in the morality of his fiction. But just as he chooses traditional narrative forms for purposes of harnessing their living potential in order to make modern chaos intelligible, so his morality is not that of traditional social and religious dogma. It is rather what John Gardner appears to mean in his book *Moral Fiction:* a celebration of life. Hence, while it is clear that for Irving (as for so many of his contemporaries) "the world *is* out of control,"[22] yet the presence of life-affirming actions and relationships remains to justify his comic-tragic vision. Love, friendship, craft, human commitment, the relationship of husband and wife, parent and child, friend and friend, writer and audience—all demand and promote ethical and moral extensions of the self, all insist on community and with community a personal and collective responsibility, all preclude the conventional judgment. Such a morality is earned, existentially arrived at; Irving works toward moral conclusions rather than from them.

This attitude evidences a willingness to examine American taboos (for example homosexuality, incest, and abortion) with openness and sympathy and ultimately to resolve the tensions that they create back into a social order compatible with traditional moral values but hardly identical with them: morality in tension with mores. But another implication is more important; despite the world's remorseless harm that, no mater how humorously treated, yet stalks the individual, Irving's fiction is free from the nihilism so characteristic of modern literature. It is this affirmation of life in the face of its clearly seen negative realities that defines his comic-tragic vision. What Warren French has said concerning the irreversible effects of modern life on the contemporary artist and the course postmodernist literature must take considering those effects, describes precisely both Irving's own awareness of the world as well as his literary program:

Once we have perceived the world as wasteland, we cannot abandon this perception, this knowledge without shutting ourselves off sentimentally from our milieu as totally as the extreme Modernists have shut themselves off distraughtly. If literature is to continue to grow and to help man to grow, it must begin to cope with the problem of accepting the culture without approving it or succumbing to it, of devising strategies by which the individual can retain his integrity without losing consciousness of his environment.[23]

The Major Themes

Virtually every Irving novel (with the possible exception of *The 158-Pound Marriage*) builds its narrative frame around the actual or attempted spiritual and intellectual growth of the major character. Indeed, the bildungsroman is Irving's principal mode of structuring his fiction, one example of his use of a traditional form to explore universal as well as new territory. This tradition is particularly evoked in his most recent novel, *The Cider House Rules.*

Embedded in the bildungsroman is, of course, almost always a dramatization of the transition from innocence to experience and the implications of that transition for the values, insights, and adult life of the developing character. While Irving's work utilizes this archetypal motif, it is symbolically and dramatically embodied in situations, characters, and places in refreshing, sometimes unique ways.

First, "innocence" may be literal and complete as the narratives begin (for example, as it is in *Garp,* John Berry of *The Hotel New Hampshire,* and Homer Wells in *The Cider House Rules*); in these cases, the family (and Irving's families are not traditional) is still the major source of guidance and support; intellectual, artistic, sexual, or profoundly emotional experience is yet to have impinged upon the character's life.

Second, Irving embodies the growth motif in older, more generally experienced characters whose innocence may be a product of emotional immaturity, a lingering impulse to maintain (or recapture) adolescent freedom, or, more central to Irving, a refusal to create, sustain, or nourish emotional commitments to others. While Trumper, protagonist of *The Water-Method Man,* is most typical of this second pattern, Graff in *Setting Free the Bears* and the unnamed narrator of *The 158-Pound Marriage* are also ripe, metaphorically and emotionally, for the initiation into meaningful experience.

One of the most vivid and effective ways Irving dramatizes these various forms of innocence is by manipulating landscape. In a variation on the symbolic use of America as virgin territory, Irving's New England—particularly isolated and rugged seashore locations—comes to be associated with youth, "family," sanctuary, the edenic place of dreams and peace. Furthermore, as growth is taking place or reality imposes itself in the forms of violence and suffering, these same pristine locations serve as psychological refuges, escapes from reality, and as places for (temporary) healing (for example, the Pillsbury Estate in *The Water-Method Man,* Dog's Head Harbor in *Garp,* the Arbuthnot-by-the-Sea in *The Hotel New Hampshire,* and Ocean View in *Cider House*).

In another conscious effort to invoke a symbolically charged landscape, Irving strategically develops a geographic metaphor through his rendering of the city of Vienna. In the first five novels, Vienna represents the place where experience is gained and mature life begins to be lived. Indeed, Irving quite directly discusses the pattern: "The reason they go to Vienna is that that's what happens when you grow up: you go to a foreign country."[24] In the work, however, that "foreign country" is very explicitly delineated as the highly particularized Vienna, and, while the complex symbolism of the place is accessible and meaningful in any single novel, the incremental effect and centrality of Vienna is most vividly apparent when one views Irving's work as a whole, or when one examines the culmination of this symbolism in *The Hotel New Hampshire.*

Much as he uses bears—an almost parodic "objective correlative"—he uses Vienna to trigger in the reader a series of associations that signal the imminence of learning in the experiential sense: Garp cannot complete his fablelike short story "The Pension Grillparzer" until he experiences the suffering and sorrow of death; John Berry will not mature until he is exposed to sexual depravity, suicide, even terrorism, all of which first occur in affective form for John, and other Irving characters, in Vienna.

Vienna as symbol, then, comes to embody the dark history of man's inhumanity to man as well as the dark recesses of individual consciousness; it often serves, in this symbolic manifestation, as a catalyst for the character's recognition of the universal nature of violence which might otherwise appear to be an exclusively American phenomenon. Irving accepts as a given the radical disorder of contemporary life, a belief he holds unequivocally despite his inherent optimism and the ability of his characters to transcend the simply nihilistic.

Another major pattern of thematic and existential significance in

Irving's work is the shaping, and gradual emergence, of female characters and the "feminine" perspective. Franny Berry, according to Irving, is the hero of *The Hotel New Hampshire*. And while one might argue that in fact the male narrator of Franny's story is ultimately the real focus of the novel, it is certainly true that as Irving's work has so far matured, his interest in creating substantial, attractive, and sympathetic female characters reflects a shift in emphasis and sensibility with significant thematic implications.

Drawn to the female victim as he reminds us Thomas Hardy was to Tess,[25] Irving admits to a kind of obsession. And while his own analogy helps explain, for example, the ubiquitousness of rape (often graphically portrayed) in Irving's narratives and the manipulative relationships that degrade the humanity of women characters, it does not explain what occurs to shift Irving's focus from "woman-as-victim" to "woman-as-hero."

In this regard, a deepening understanding and interpretation of human nature seems increasingly to inform Irving's vision, an interpretation that recognizes the possiblity of—indeed, in the last three novels suggests the necessity for—the integration of the traditionally "feminine" and "masculine" into the coherent whole of the mature self. Apparently utterly sympathetic with the fundamental perspective of feminism, Irving nevertheless savagely exposes its excesses (particularly in his treatment of the self-flagellating Ellen Jamesians in *Garp*) in order to provide a platform for what emerges as a genuinely androgynous vision.

Eschewing political rhetoric, Irving develops his life-affirming and most memorable characters into those whose lives and values most clearly represent a fusion of traditional female/male attitudes and activities. His sensitive and enduring men love and care for children; they encourage the full and independent development of their female counterparts; they view rape as the ultimate violation of human values, and abortion—though fraught with profound moral dilemmas—as ultimately a humane act. For the most part, this growth is not created in representational terms or through abstractions in Irving's work, but is embodied in dramatic situations, characters, and actions that make concrete what is too frequently in contemporary literature unassimilated rhetorical material.

Roberta Muldoon in *Garp,* for example, represents the literal state of androgynous integration the way only a transsexual can in human experience. But because she is an anomaly, Irving replays the transsexual experience by having Garp attend Jenny's funeral in drag and subsequently experience the victimizing world, albeit briefly, through the perspective of a woman. These ever-less literal androgynous episodes and images form the metaphoric backdrop against which Garp and Helen's experience must finally be evaluated. The "male" possessiveness and outrage (despite Garp's own record of infidelity) that leads to their son Walt's death will be mitigated in the reconciliation between husband and wife. That reconciliation, as defined by the life-engendering commitment to produce and adopt other children as well as simultaneously to pursue independent careers and mutually supportive lives, creates the tenuously balanced androgynous whole. The murder of Garp by a psychotic Ellen Jamesian ironically underscores the transitory nature of the human, and in this case, transcendent and androgynous state and reemphasizes the destructive nature of political fanaticism, whatever its guise.

It takes Irving four novels of experimentation with the androgyny theme before he embodies it successfully, perhaps before his artistic and personal vision perceive it clearly enough. His fifth novel reinforces the theme and unravels it in other unconventional ways, most notably in the treatment of John and Franny's incest, while in his most recent novel the implications of androgyny are felt in the lives of both major characters, Dr. Larch and the orphan Homer Wells.

Life and Art

No matter how often Irving himself, or his characters, reject the contemporary obsession with "fiction about fiction," Irving is nevertheless a writer who repeatedly explores—either literally or metaphorically—the several, sometimes paradoxical, relationships of art to life. Moreover, Irving engages in this exploration with such skill that while he transcends the world accessible to the reader of popular literature, he does so without disturbing the narrative line that attracts the average reader in the first place.

Beginning with the roughly integrated journals of *Setting Free the Bears* and posing the problems of historian, journalist, historical novelist, and filmmaker in his first three novels, Irving repeatedly demonstrates his fascination with the subject of art's value, function, and human significance. But his fascination is not Barthian; indeed, however profoundly treated, it is always integrated with the narrative thrust and, in *Garp,* is brilliantly subsumed by the unfolding human drama.

The relationships of art to life and the ways in which the artist uses his own experience as the basis for his narratives is a recurring thematic problem posed by various Irving artist protagonists. Trumper, for example, helps create a film that ultimately reveals to him the meaningless pattern of his life by objectifying his experience; he also recognizes how his "translation" of the "old low Norse" ballad is actually a form of therapy rather than a legitimate academic exercise— an unhealthy exercise because art must have its own integrity and cannot perform a purely therapeutic function if it is to be successful as art. Likewise, Garp's best work, represented by the short story "The Pension Grillparzer," is a superb piece because it utilizes the delicately shaped products of the imagination and integrates them into a significant symbolic whole. While it is true that Garp, the artist, is unable to complete the fable until he experiences the suffering and death of another human being, the story itself is not a direct reflection of that experience at all, but an embodiment of the human condition portrayed through a phantasmagoric prism.

Later Garp *will* undergo a personal exorcism and use art as a vehicle for that exorcism: "The World According to Bensenhaver" is a shocking and effective piece, and while it clearly represents Garp's attempt to come to terms with his tragic experience, it also reveals the ways in which an artist can shape and control materials that, in their unassimilated and unstructured form, would be profoundly destructive to his emotional well-being.

In addition to the ever-elusive subject of literature's relationship to life, Irving also explores other questions about the nature and function of art. In *Setting Free the Bears* and *The 158-Pound Marriage,* for instance, he poses an almost Faulknerian paradox regarding the ways in which history, art, and even action, intersect and thereby inform experience. Graff presents Siggy's journals to reflect the rationale for freeing the animals from the Hietzinger Zoo, but in so doing, he also presents a "pre-history," which is far more interesting and illuminating; as a key to the spiritual malaise that characterizes Vienna and will ultimately dictate the city's response to the "zoo-bust," Siggy's interpretation of the past is inextricably bound by the present in ways of which Graff is only dimly aware.

The narrator of *Marriage* is, by profession, an historical novelist who prides himself in understanding the appropriate dynamic that links historical data and the materials of the imagination. But his blindness to the meaning of the personal histories of the three other principals in the novel leads him to misinterpret emotional cues and sensibilities and finally to lose everything that is important to him. The naive conviction that experience can be determined solely in the present and will not carry with it the emotional baggage of the past creates the final irony of the novel: that an historical novelist holds this conviction represents a further irony and indicates once again how central the issues raised by art are to Irving's work.

In Irving's latest novel, *The Cider House Rules,* the reader discovers an elaborate web of references to Dickens, Charlotte Brontë, and the nineteenth-century novel, which must be called modestly self-reflexive. More important, much of the plot turns on a doctor-as-artist trope; Larch "creates" Homer and (although the character temporarily escapes his author) he ultimately "writes" Homer's life into its final configuration. Once again, the metaphor of artist serves to embody the creative impulses that are the only weapons human beings have at their disposal to deal with the otherwise destructive forces that define experience.

"Lunacy and Sorrow": The Comic-Tragic Vision

In T. S. Garp's most successful fiction, "The Pension Grillparzer," the narrator muses over a narrative by "a storyteller who is accepting of unhappy endings," finding it difficult to understand her "curious lack of either enthusiasm or bitterness" (180). In a limited sense Irving's own fiction is the literature of acceptance; he writes about— without feeling he can really change—the universal wrongness of life. In a more important sense, however, such acceptance neither can be, nor is accompanied by, the unquestioning neutrality that surprises the narrator of "The Pension Grillparzer." Irving reacts to the world as it is (and as it will be) as a fabulist, not a realist; his is the vision of "lunacy and sorrow," of comedy and tragedy. He has denied being an "essayist" or a "reporter" carefully observing ugly fragments of reality; what he claims interests him in the novel is that "it's a whole dream of life."[26] The comedy and the tragedy are one.

His novels abound in scenes both painful and amusing, and in a like manner Garp's fiction responds to life's inescapable duality. It is in response to a reader's outrage at what she sees as Garp's humor

achieved at the expense of the wounded that Irving most lucidly articulates this vision. When Mrs. I. B. Poole of Findlay, Ohio, writes
Garp to accuse him of gross insensitivity to the suffering of others,
Garp enters into an epistolary debate which ends in frustrated and
mutual recrimination. Garp, admitting that his "laughter is pretty
desperate," attempts to explain through parable and direct statement
the essential nature of laughter. For Mrs. Poole's

letter stung Garp like a slap; rarely had he felt so importantly misunder-
stood. Why did people insist that if you were "comic" you couldn't also be
"serious"? Garp felt most people confused being profound with being sober,
being earnest with being deep. Apparently, if you *sounded* serious, you were.
Presumably, other animals could not laugh at themselves, and Garp believed
that laughter was related to sympathy, which we were always needing more
of. He had been, after all, a humorless child—and never religious—so perhaps he now took comedy more seriously than others.
  But for Garp to see his vision interpreted as making *fun* of people was
painful to him; and to realize that his art had made him appear cruel gave
Garp a keen sense of failure. (232)

When Garp, baffled by his inability to convince the philistine, ends
the exchange with a two word letter—"Fuck you"—the omniscient
narrator quietly observes that thus was Garp's "sense of humor lost,
and his sympathy taken from the world" (237). The beauty of "The
Pension Grillparzer" was, in fact, that it "had somehow struck the
chord of comedy (on the one hand) and compassion (on the other)"
(237). That Garp's humor had neither cheapened nor sentimentalized
his characters' lives justified the fiction's existence and accounted for,
in the narrator's view, its excellence.
  What Marilyn French calls Irving's preoccupation with "the terrifying contingency of human life," in which "the great equalizer is
death and its harbinger, accident,"[27] is embodied in refrains throughout his novels. In *Setting Free the Bears* the narrator learns to dread
"the gale of the world"; in *The World According to Garp* the danger is
represented by the sleepless "Under Toad"; in *The Hotel New Hampshire* the characters who survive must "keep passing the open windows"; in *Cider House Rules* a chief rule is to "wait and see."
  As Garp's murder in the very womblike security of his wrestling
room suggests, even the strong and wary will eventually pause too
long and hence confront the inevitable destruction. But unlike the
bleak fiction of some so-called postmodernists, with whom humor is

always black and produces only the chilling laughter of negation, Irving's fiction moves us again and again to what a character in *The Hotel New Hampshire* calls "happy fatalism." The comedy of *The World According to Garp* is "life-affirming," Irving has argued, "even though everybody dies."[28]

Perhaps he should have said *because* everybody dies. For with a few exceptions, the comic-tragic view of this reality pervades Irving's fiction, from the bizarre death of Siggy Javotnik in *Setting Free the Bears* to the multiple grotesqueries of *The Hotel New Hampshire*. Something of this attitude is explained in the following passage from the latter novel. John Berry, the narrator, describes the family philosophy:

The way the world worked was *not* cause for some sort of blanket cynicism or sophomoric despair; according to my father and Iowa Bob, the way the world worked—which was badly—was just a strong incentive to live purposefully, and to be determined about living well. . . .

And one night, when we were watching a wretched melodrama on the TV above the bar in the Hotel New Hampshire, my mother said, "I don't want to see the end of this. I like happy endings."

And Father said, "There are no happy endings."

"Right!" cried Iowa Bob—an odd mixture of exuberance and stoicism in his cracked voice. "Death is horrible, final, and frequently premature," Coach Bob declared.

"So what?" my father said.

"Right!" cried Iowa Bob. "That's the point: so what?" (168)

There is a nakedness of perspective here, a certain refusal that invites criticism for being naive or sentimental. It is to Irving's credit that he accepts the danger; fiction, he argues, "should produce laughter and tears" and to achieve that end "a writer has to risk vulnerability."[29]

It is significant that readers are frequently reminded of Dickens, quite literally in *The Cider House Rules,* when assessing Irving's work; Dickens, too, risked popularity and, with it, vulnerability. What Eleanor Wymard has said of Irving applies to Dickens as well; both "reveal the complexity of human existence from the generous perspective of comedy." For Irving's Garp, she points out, "the comic spirit is the courage to endure, in the middle of spring, the experience of pain and tragedy."[30]

Just as tragedy, in its traditional sense, dignifies the human experience through shared suffering, so comedy, too, has generally been positive. Whatever has been the fate of humor in post-war fiction, however it may freeze empathy or even deny its very existence, Irving, as John Gardner has said, is one of those writers "whose humor never snipes with mere cruelty";[31] the woman from Findlay, Ohio, is wrong. It is in the affirmative nature of Irving's comic-tragic vision that his very essence may be found.

Chapter Two

Setting Free the Bears: From "Pre-History" to Fiction

Irving's *Setting Free the Bears* possesses the classic qualities of a first novel by a talented but undeveloped writer: major weaknesses, signs of imitation and moments of unqualified literary success. Its major weaknesses include the failure of its principal characters to emerge as well-defined and developed personages, the unsureness of its structure, and the fuzziness and uncertainty of its theme. As a "road" novel—that identifiably American version of the ancient picaresque— it reminds us of what the young Irving had been reading in the 1960s, as do the occasional passages of Dylan Thomas-like prose. But clearly transcending these inadequacies are indications of genuine novelistic strength: richly drawn scenes, moments of history intensely evoked, passages of prose already marked by a highly personal and remarkably effective style. And for all the novel's uncertainty of attitude, Irving here first yokes the comic and the serious, the bizarre and the meaningful, but without the full control over this dangerous and characteristic juxtaposition that he will achieve in later novels. Thus one detects the emerging outline of a yet to be realized vision, occasionally embodied in a very personal mode. Although the novel must finally be judged a critical failure on major points, it can be seen to be more than simply an interesting entertainment. To the student of his later work, much that here both succeeds and fails points ahead to, and helps clarify, the mature fiction. Moreover, a significant portion of the novel can be justified on its own merits.

"Living off the Land"

Setting Free the Bears is divided into three sections, the first of which tells of the mobile adventures of two dropouts from the University of Vienna, while the last describes the culmination of these events after the death of one of the students. The central section—by far the most interesting and well-written part—consists of portions chosen from two journals kept by the dead student: a "zoo watch" containing his detailed observations on nocturnal conditions in Vienna's Heitzinger Zoo and his "highly selective autobiography," which he also calls his "pre-history."

Part one of the novel, which takes place in the spring of 1967, is set in Vienna and the Austrian countryside. Two of its three principal characters are Hannes Graff, come from a vague past in Salzburg to study at the University of Vienna, and Sigfried ("Siggy") Javotnik, child in a very literal sense of the recent upheaval in Europe in general and Austria and Yugoslavia in particular. When the two meet both have suffered academic failure and, in a moment of recognized affinity, they buy "an old, cruel-looking motorcycle," a Royal Enfield 700 cc. "lovely like a gun" (7), and set out to explore the world—at least, that is, as far as the coast of Italy.

Before leaving a city clearly repugnant to their youth and vitality, Siggy urges a visit to the zoo, which Hannes gladly accepts. There we are introduced to, among others, three of the animals that eventually take on symbolic or even mythic significance in the novel: the Asiatic Black Bear, the Rare Spectacled Bears, and the Oryx. And while still at the zoo, Siggy and Hannes cavort with two local girls whose very different natures seem also to hint at symbolic meaning.

Siggy, dedicated to the classically youthful dream of freedom so much a part of the road novel, insists on three rules: "no planning," "pick roads that the beast will love," and "travel light" (9–10). But once on the road they discover that when "one is to live off the land . . . there are certain investments required" (28). Early on an amiable farmer with whom they have exchanged their freshly caught trout for a breakfast, turns out to be a game warden and fines them fifty schillings for exceeding the bag limit. Other adventures occur, as when they are assaulted by a hostile and neurotic homosexual; but the story at this stage is meant to be lighthearted and its pattern is characterized by the narrator's comment: "so we left for the next town" (34). However, very soon Siggy's release of goats penned behind a *gasthaus* offers a microcosm of the zoo bust yet to come. That his actions result in more, not less, unpleasantness for the goats clearly foretells the outcome of the later action. But as Siggy sees it, the problem results from the cowardice of long domesticated animals, not from the plan itself.

When the two drifters pick up a shy and lovely girl called Gallen, the primary cast of the main narrative is complete. Her wariness of the bike's other passengers eventually causes Hannes (who at this point has yet to learn to drive) to burn his calves seriously on the tail pipes; the story enters a new phase when he is taken to the girl's aunt's *gasthaus* to be healed of his painful wounds. Hannes is genuinely smitten with the girl, but Siggy's mind is now increasingly fixed on plans for the zoo animals' liberation. When Siggy attacks a drunken milkman for savagely beating his horse and is forced to flee, he apparently plans to return later for Hannes. Siggy uses the occasion, however, to return to Vienna in order to reconnoiter the zoo; Hannes uses it to pursue Gallen.

When Siggy returns at night to reclaim Hannes from the village authorities who have forced him to take a job bringing in full beehives from the hillside orchards in order to pay rent and damages, he crashes the old Enfield under a wagon loaded with hives; he is apparently stung to death and Hannes receives enough toxin to be made once again an invalid in the *gasthaus*. He spends his second recovery by reading Siggy's journal made while scouting the zoo, and studying his informal family history.

The second section of *Setting Free the Bears* tells an altogether more complicated and interesting story. Hannes, sick not only from multiple bee stings but also with guilt at having failed his friend, reads and edits Siggy's journals, interweaving segments of the recent zoo account with others drawn from the "pre-history." The zoo journal is thematically related to Siggy's history; in it he uncovers the systematic torture of the animals by a night watchman named O. Schrutt, a former Nazi. The presence of Schrutt politicizes the situation by linking it to Europe's sick past and it adds some small justification for the otherwise quixotic attempt. Nevertheless it remains largely a madcap adventure and, by comparison, the personal history is far more complex and engrossing, detailing as it does the Austrian background of Siggy's mother and her family and the Yugoslavian origins of his father. This serio-comic account concludes with the family's postwar experience.

The Austrian sequence begins in May 1935, but concentrates on 1938, the year of the *Anschluss* forced by Hitler on a demoralized Austria. Hilke Marter and her student boyfriend, the politically minded Zahn Glanz, court amidst the largely incomprehensible tensions of prewar Austria. Walking together in Vienna's Rathaus Park, they discover a small, deranged squirrel with "a pink and perfect, hairless swastika carved on its head" (109). On Radio Johannesgasse they hear of suspicious deaths, of old men—presumably Jews—chased into the paths of trams by gangs of youths, of a young woman, fully clothed except for her stockings, found murdered by a "star-shaped series of five-pointed stab wounds in the heart" (120) and hung by her coat in a wardrobe closet of the Vienna State Opera during a performance of *Lohengrin*. Such is the decadence of an ancient nation drifting into chaos. But mainly they watch and discuss with Hilke's father, a patriotic and independently minded old librarian, the ensuing fall of Austria; Siggy's journals detail the last days of the regime of Chancellor Kurt von Schuschnigg, who, though himself pro-German, tries unsuccessfully to keep his country free of Nazi domination. When Hitler betrays his earlier assurance of nonaggression and forces Schuschnigg to cancel a plebiscite to determine Austria's independence or unification with Germany, Hilke's family, along with a remarkable old chicken farmer, Ernst Watzek-Trummer, but without Zahn Glanz, flee to the rural village of Kaprun. Watzek-Trummer had previously endeared himself to the Marter family by his patriotism; constructing an Austrian eagle costume out of tin pie plates and chicken feathers, he had stormed Vienna crying "*Cawk! Cawk!* Austria is free!" (126). Like grandfather Marter, however, he knows the nation lacks political will and is hence doomed.

The story of Siggy's Yugoslavian father, Vratno Javotnik, is more complex and deadly. A Croat or a Slovene but not a Serb, he was that most unusual of Yugoslavs—one for whom tribal background meant nothing: "his politics were strictly personal . . . he had no affiliations" (157). His story starts in 1941 when, as Germany invades his country, he leaves the University of Zagreb where he had studied languages. Eventually ending up in Slovenjgradec, he makes survival his business by attempting to steer clear of the Germans, the Serbian resistance fighters called Chetniks, the communist partisans, and the Ustashi terrorist organization which, though criminally rather than politically motivated, supports the invading Germans. But in Slovenjgradec he is forced to assist the sinister Slivnica family, employed by the Ustashi, in their complicated attempts to implicate criminally and later assassinate Gottlob Wut, a former motorcycle genius of questionable ethics and presently the scout-outfit leader of Motorcycle Unit Balkan Four.

Vratno gains the friendship of Wut by pleading for his help in reacquiring motorcycle skills supposedly lost after a relative was killed in a dramatic crash. But when the time comes for him to kill Wut, Vratno warns him of the Ustashi plans instead and the two escape into the mountains on a pair of stolen German motorcycles. They spend the remainder of the war, like Siggy and Hannes, "living off the land," but in an altogether more precarious fashion. Eventually Wut is recognized by his old comrades and summarily executed in a most grotesque fashion. Vratno—who abandons his friend in his moment of need when the instinct for survival overcomes him—escapes on one of the bikes, a 1939 Grand Prix racer. With forged papers and a German uniform, he gets to Vienna and, almost psychotic with fear ("war paranoia," Watzek-Trummer calls it), he hides in the Marter's former apartment to escape the invading Russian army. He is found there by the Marters on their return and the rest of the "pre-history" describes their lives under Russian occupation.

Hilke marries Vratno in lieu of the still missing Zahn Glanz and, on the night Siggy is born, a trigger-happy Russian soldier machine guns Hilke's mother as she rushes to the window to shout the good news. In escaping from his Ustashi enemies Wut had killed the Slivnica family by rolling a hand grenade under their car; the "terrible Todor, body-awesome" family leader, had survived, however, and tracing Vratno to Vienna murders Siggy's young father in revenge. The remaining Marters return to Kaprun, grieving over Grandmother Marter's death and Vratno's assassination. Hilke, still hoping to find her prewar boyfriend Zahn Glanz, returns alone to Vienna and disappears. Finally defeated, old Marter takes a mail sled up into the mountains above the village and, dressed in Watzek-Trummer's battered eagle suit, makes a suicidal run down the Catapult Trail, dying in a snowdrift as a result. Siggy's story told, we only now learn that he had been a history major at the university, but that his thesis—this engrossing "pre-history"—had been rejected because it lacked scholarly documentation.

The novel's short concluding section tells how, after Siggy's body has been shipped to Watzek-Trummer in Kaprun for burial, the recuperated Hannes escapes with Gallen from her aunt's *gasthaus* on the repaired Enfield, aided by the bearlike Keff. On the road once more and camping in the mountains, Hannes and Gallen at last consummate their love affair. Despite this long-desired event, and despite the realization that Siggy's plans for the zoo bust are impossible and probably insane, a guilt-ridden Hannes takes Gallen to Vienna ostensibly to get jobs but actually because he has assumed Siggy's obsession. Gallen sells her lovely long hair (signaling her loss of innocence) and reluctantly accompanies Hannes to the Heitzinger Zoo where, rejecting his promise to release only a few harmless animals, he actually frees most of the beasts, causing a bloody chaos to ensue. Many animals are killed, including the marvelous Oryx with his symbolically huge testicles, and eventually the survivors will be rounded up. Hannes and Gallen escape the confusion and when they stop along the highway she leaves him to return to the city, refusing to indicate whether or not she will meet him some evening in the Vienna woods. Hannes sets out on the motorcycle for Kaprun to find Watzek-Trummer, the Marter family historian, and tell him the final story. He has pulled himself together and rides "properly balanced," indicating that perhaps now he can straighten out his life. And just before he mounts the bike to leave, in a moment of possibly symbolic justification for his quixotic act, he sees the two Rare Spectacled Bears moving purposefully over the fields, side by side.

Comic, Satiric, Grotesque

Despite its length, like all such exercises the above summary is very incomplete—all the more since Irving's novels are generally congested, and this one—written in the picaresque tradition—is especially so. But more important, this description only hints at the tone of the novel. The peculiarly Irvingesque serio-comic tone that culminates in *The World According to Garp,* is continued in *The Hotel New Hampshire* and, to a lesser degree, in *Cider House,* is first attempted here, though without the clear mastery that marks later books. In this sense as in others, *Bears* is the young novelist's workshop. Several elements of this crucial tone are already present: a feeling of pure comic joy in the most positive sense, an ironic-satiric strand, moments of the outright grotesque—all intermingled with serious thought and genuine sentiment. This complex tone will become the hallmark of Irving's fiction and carry the burden of his peculiar vision; Garp will meditate on the serious nature of comedy and the novel of which he is the hero will provide the extreme example. In *Bears,* however, Irving seems to have begun with a less complicated intention, however ambiguous the novel may actually have turned out.

The ironies are directed, somewhat imprecisely, at Siggy's cockeyed plan to free the animals, at Hannes's rationalizations as he assumes Siggy's role, at Gallen's touching naïveté. It assumes its most aggressive, hard-edged form, however, in its larger treatment of society—the present and past conduct of human affairs. Events leading up to the pre–World War II *Anschluss*, for example, are marked by what has even been called Irving's cynicism, though this may be the wrong term to describe his icy anger at the spectacle of Austrian ineptitude and failure of purpose on one side, and Nazi unscrupulousness on the other. Irving watches the debacle through Grandfather Marter and his family, a man who uses irony as a tool of survival. We see a well-intentioned Chancellor Schuschnigg try to ride out the growing storm by taking one step backward after another. Germany, headed by Hitler and manipulated by his disciples, is implacable and Irving's irony is bitter: "Göring has such an odd way of putting things. He promises that Austria will have German military *aid,* if the Schuschnigg government cannot change itself promptly" (143).

Indeed, the state of affairs in Austria just before Hitler invades seems to deserve the special mixture of tones that Irving appears to prefer. We watch the single guard of honor outside the chancellery scratch his back with his bayonetted and probably unloaded rifle, while inside ensues a sort of Gilbert and Sullivan political sequence. Yet the "old and small . . . and dead" Jew "caught in the gale" (115) and killed by a roving gang of youths is seen to be only a forerunner; 76,000 people in Vienna alone will be swept up in the first wave of Gestapo arrests. Irving's logic is clear: the *Anschluss* is part of a continuity leading to the holocaust. This realization is both comically and terribly illustrated by the parallel zoo journal; as the events of 1938 are being reported in 1969, Siggy is learning more about the night guard in the zoo, a former Nazi whose postwar appetite for cruelty takes the form of torturing small, helpless animals. The emergence of O. Schrutt and the gangs of violent Hitler toughs juxtaposed against Chancellor Schuschnigg's failure of nerve illustrate Irving's endorsement of those lines in William Butler Yeats's "The Second Coming" that most tellingly describe the predicament of modern history: "The best lack all conviction, while the worst / Are full of passionate intensity." Actually, Schrutt restricts his "atrocities" enough so that, with his exaggerated, paramilitary uniform and behavior, he is more comic than sinister. Yet when Schrutt is himself trapped by an avenging Hannes and groveling in fear, he recites the names of long-dead Jews who he fears have somehow returned from the horror of which he had been a part to exact their understandably terrible revenge. He is amusing, but the entire experience that he represents is deadly.

The Yugoslavian sequence offers a similar tonal duality but, though the Slivnica family and Gottlob Wut provide genuine humor, the horror is more immediate. Vratno Javotnik does not just step backward; he runs, "preparing for his sly survival" (159). His is a world of absolute chaos, a world without the mitigating generosity and familial love of the Marter family. Instead, the Slivnicas offer a deadly antitype in which hate, greed, and brutality replace love, generosity, and consolation. Everywhere in this world one finds betrayal and internecine conflict: "there were too many side wars within the war" (187), a catastrophic fragmentation of human integrity. Colonel Drazha Mihailovich and his wild Chetniks bravely harass the Germans, but they in turn are hunted by Tito's communists whose savage annihilation of these heroic nationalists is hidden under superior propaganda. Reprisal killings by the Germans and their Ustashi allies run into the thousands and the fleeing Vratno and Wut are forced to witness human nature at its most brutal:

My father would always remember a raft snagged in some deadfall along the bank. The raft was neatly piled with heads: the architect had attempted a pyramid. It was almost perfect. But one head near the peak had slipped out of place; its hair was caught between other heads, and it swung from face to face in the river wind; some faces watched the swinging, and some looked away. My father and Gottlob again drove back to the Slovenian mountains, near the village of Rogla, and that night slept in each other's arms. (198)

There is nothing humorous about this description (unless it is the concluding "babes in the woods" image) but it illustrates a grotesque quality that does extend the novel's frame of reference and influences its tone. For example, the death of Siggy beneath the wagon load of bees—Siggy whose shiny head has been shaved utterly bald in an absurd attempt at disguise—is accompanied by the funny but dreadful sound of "THANG!" and the entire scene has the quality of a cartoon character's lethal accident, but without the miraculous recovery. Siggy's naked assault on the drunken milkman earlier, during which Hannes birches Siggy's bare buttocks and Siggy literally runs down a pompous burgher, offers a more innocent version of Irving's skill at creating bizarre scenes. The latter scene embodies the tone apparently

intended for the entire novel—Siggy's intentions are good and despite
the pain nothing terrible develops—while the former scene suggests
the way comedy, and hence tone, can get out of hand in this work.

Siggy's death produces a change in the novel by making way for
the larger social and political concerns that dominate the family
chronicle, his "pre-history." Grandmother's death, Wut's death,
Vratno's death—each is violent, unnecessary and yet, in some perverse way, funny. The machine gunning of Grandmother Marter reminds us of the emotional dangers encountered when one witnesses
an old woman slip on a banana peel; sympathy and concern are called
for but unseemly laughter threatens. Wut is assassinated in an out-
door toilet by his former motorcycle troopers; in a mad scene he is
upended and sent "head-first down into the breathless bog [of the la-
trine]. Balkan 4 worked as a team" (212). Vratno's death is not directly described, but his assassin, the terrible Todor, demonstrates
what has occurred by bringing his huge fist down on a scoop of cus-
tard trembling in his hand; the resultant sticky fragmentation makes
Vratno's end perfectly clear. "Todor, among other things, was known
for his sense of humor" (241). So, we might add, is Irving.

But perhaps the paramount example of confused intention and ambiguous tone is the zoo bust itself. Initially Hannes's act of liberation
is to be symbolic—only a few harmless animals and, for the libera-
tors, "the rarest of fun" (32). Increasingly, however, Hannes is preoccupied with punishing O. Schrutt; he has read the journals and,
despite his realization that Siggy was unbalanced, recognizes and accepts Siggy's equation: the forces that tyrannized Austria-Yugoslavia
are miniaturized in the zoo-as-concentration-camp. And Hannes by
now suffers a two-fold guilt: by leaving Salzburg he and his family
had missed the war and, like Vratno with whom he now seems—
perhaps unconsciously—to identify, he had abandoned his friend. He
worries that he "might be going mad. Or just bizarre" (293).

What starts out, then, in the free and easy picaresque comedy of
part one can only be finished after Siggy's largely unexpected and certainly grotesque death and the very moving disclosures of his personal
history in an entirely darker world. And like the pattern of the novel
itself, the zoo bust moves from a youthful lark (a classic confrontation
between the high spirits and love of freedom of youth and the world
of restraint and baffled power symbolized by the zoo) to a scene of
death and destruction: the joke turned tragic. Releasing the goats at
the *gasthaus* had been ineffectual but fun; releasing the animals frees

only madness. The scene, no longer funny but nonetheless filled with
terrible energy, rises to a crescendo of violence:

I found my poor Gallen huddled in the doorway aisle of the maze, watching
down the blood-bathed path to where a tiger, his stripes tinted crimson and
black in the infrared, was squatting over a large and tawny, deep-chested
antelope with spiraled horns; with a large brain-shaped mass of intestines
spilled over his side. And with a hind hoof bent or drawn up under his
thigh, over which sprawled his unmistakable, familiar balloons of volleyball
size. (327)

Even the marvelous Oryx, symbol of procreative energy and totem of
these young males on the loose, has fallen victim.

"At Loose Ends"

In some of the strongest writing of the novel outside the "pre-
history," Irving evokes the drastically changed mood and tone of the
novel as he describes the final zoo scenes. Totally out of control now,
the animals suggest not so much the Darwinian jungle as a riot in a
death camp. Hannes, whose own control has been gradually eroded
since Siggy's loss, is no longer the man with "a plan":

"You're free to go!" I screamed. "Why don't you? Don't ask for too
much!" And responding to my voice was what sounded like the utter demol-
ishment of the *Biergarten*. I pelted down there, through a crunchy dust of
littered ashtrays. This was a primate sort of destruction, for sure; a vandalism
of a shocking, human type. They had shattered the one-time funhouse mirror; chunks of it lay all over the *Biergarten* terrace. I kept looking down at
my puzzlework reflection, looming over myself. (325)

The imagery of the fragmented mirror beautifully represents Hannes's
own disintegration, accelerated now by events beyond his control but
always an element in the novel's theme. As the final action had begun, Hannes believed himself to be in "total charge"; he had seen
every animal in the zoo as passive victims "awaiting Hannes Graff's
decision" (321). But the climactic chapter that follows these words is
entitled "my reunion with the real and unreasonable world" (321),
and Hannes must come to grips not only with reality but with himself. We now recognize what Siggy meant in his notebook entry made
on the day that he first met Hannes: "He's a nice person. At loose

ends, though" (265), a description that will fit many of Irving's later
male characters, especially Trumper in the next novel, *The Water-
Method Man*. This has been, in fact, the story of the narrator's be-
mused search for himself, a sort of bildungsroman.

Drifting to Vienna out of an indeterminate past, Hannes had increasingly identified with, as well as followed, the eccentric Siggy.
After Siggy's death the journals had insinuated, for Hannes, not only
the absence of purpose but a negative model in the guilty Vratno, a
decent man who yet lacks all conviction and abandons a friend; Hannes's instinctive, unconscious identification with Vratno is a logical
result of his vague feeling of responsibility in Siggy's death. The
chaos of the zoo bust replicates the chaos of Yugoslavia during the
war. Just as Vratno, before his rehabilitation by the Marters, is left a
shattered "war paranoid," so Hannes is reduced now to mental inco-
herence and largely blind action. But trauma cannot blot out the full
horror of his failure. Not only has animal violence been the result of
his absurd intervention; more terrible still is the emergence of the
"primate sort of destruction" that now develops and begins to mo-
nopolize his dread. In his hallucination he sees an atavistic vision:

But in the Tiroler Garten there was also a crowd, a pre-dawn army of
more citizens than police—of suburb folk in nightwear, blinking flashlights.
We were not noticed in the mayhem; we jogged alongside housewives,
shriller than monkeys.

It was only when we reached the larger, darker shrubs of Maxing Park,
that a sense of outcome loomed clearly in my mind against his chaos.
Through the shrubs, I saw them hiding. Anonymous men with ancient
weapons—with fireplace tridents, grub hoes and gleaming bucksaws; pitch-
forks, sledges and moon-shaped sickles. And *people's* voices, now, were raised
above the Asiatic Black Bear's din—left behind me. (329)

Some things are more terrible than zoos.

Near the novel's end, then, Hannes comes to recognize a new danger. He has intervened in the nature of things and failed. One result
is the defection of Gallen—whether permanent or not he cannot
know. Another is the possiblity that, like John Barth's protagonist in
The End of the Road, he may be paralyzed, rendered incapable of action. Fleeing the zoo on the bike, he feels the anguished Gallen's
teeth in his shoulder and wishes "for all this world that she could bite
much deeper and hurt me more" (331). Once safely escaped into the
countryside he feels himself running down:

Hannes Graff, I thought, is too split-haired and loose-ended to ever rise up out of this road ditch and ride his beastly motorcycle out of this deceptively ordered countryside.

And orderly, too, were the towns I'd go through. If only I could get myself started.

• • •

But what deadened me in the road ditch was that *none* of my ideas was very stirring, and there seemed to be no excitable planning called for—for *this* trip.

Something new to get used to, I thought. How Hannes Graff was rendered inert. (336–37)

Unlike Barth's character, the immediate cause of his paralysis is new guilt piled on the old. "What worse awareness is there than to know there would have been a better outcome if you'd never done anything at all? That all small mammals would have been better off if you'd never meddled in the unsatisfactory scheme of things" (337). But the actions leading up to that mental state reflect a failure of self-realization, an absence of any volitional center. Unlike Gallen who knows what she wants (to love Hannes, to live in Vienna), he has more nearly reacted than acted, and now even that may be impossible.

Because Hannes's inertness is so clearly described only four pages from the novel's conclusion, and so fully embodies the logic of his character, the reader has the right to question the book's final and, it would seem, ambiguous implications. As Hannes tries to convince himself to leave for Kaprun, there to put himself in the hands of old Watzek-Trummer—that genuine survivor—the gentle pair of Rare Spectacled Bears appears, running purposefully side by side toward some destination only they can know. Thankful for, and encouraged by, their escape (probably the only animals to make one), he mounts the big motorcycle and very carefully attempts to start. Step by step, in a deliberate though clumsy fashion, he proceeds; "the point is, everything worked" (340). He can now claim that he will admit responsibility for the zoo deaths and commit himself to the judgment of Watzek-Trummer, "the keeper of details." Then, in imagery crucial to Irving's personal experience and imagination, he can ride the bike:

So I felt the clutch in my left hand; I controlled the throttle and front brake with my right. I put myself in gear and was properly balanced when I came out of the gravel at the roadside. I was steady, shifting up, when I

rode into the full-force wind. But I didn't panic; I leaned to the curves; I
held the crown of the road and drove faster and faster. I truly outdrove the
wind. For sure—for the moment, at least—there was no gale hurrying me
out of this world.
   For sure, Siggy, I'll have to let your grave mound grow a little grass.
   For sure, Gallen, I'll look you up some Wednesday.
   For sure, I expect to hear great things of the Rare Spectacled Bears. (340)

   And so the novel concludes. But has Irving earned the optimism
implied here? Taken at its face value, but especially in Irving's world,
motorcycle skills offer a metaphor for self-control and maturation.
Yet mastery of the old bike also links Hannes—ominously and ines-
capably—with the dead cyclists: the madly idealistic Siggy, the sly
survivalist Vratno, possibly even the equivocal Wut. Even before the
zoo affair Hannes had come to recognize that, at the end, Siggy was
"totally paranoid" (275) and as for Vratno, that "war paranoid," Hannes himself had all too readily learned to dream "the coward's dream
of impossible isolation" (273) which had deluded Siggy's father.
   Gabriel Miller believes that "Hannes has assimilated the lessons of
history" and that, as a result, the novel's "ending suggests that his
education will have positive effects. He has learned what life will have
in store for him and about the finality of death."[1] But if Irving's attempt has been to write a bildungsroman here, and it seems clear that
he has, are we convinced that Hannes *has* matured? Or are his skills,
like those of Vratno, his spiritual father, skills of evasion and his trip
to Watzek-Trummer only the holding action of one who lacks all conviction? The repeated "for sure" (used four times in the last few sentences of the novel) implies more nearly uncertainty than confidence.
And it is not clear that he has come at last to understand Siggy's
meditation on his family's past, or that he recognizes the difference
between what is the inevitable shape of human destiny[2] and what the
individual can alter. Moreover, despite the deaths of most of the major characters, there is little indication that Hannes truly understands
the finalty of death. In addition, the imagery of the novel's concluding passage as easily can be taken to imply the desire for escape as it
can Hannes's ability to move purposefully forward: "I didn't panic; I
leaned to the curves; I held the crown of the road and drove faster
and faster." For him to say "I truly outdrove the wind . . . there was
no gale hurrying me out of this world" is dangerous; as all of Irving's
fiction will come to demonstrate, the gale of the world never stops
blowing for long.

"The Gale of the World"

The task of determining the significance of the novel's conclusion or, for that matter, the rest of the work, is complicated by the weakness of both Hannes and Siggy as characters. Siggy is the novel's main source of past experience and the stimulus of present action, and Hannes is its first person narrator; both are therefore critical. Yet in execution and probably in concept they are flawed.

There is, for instance, a radical discrepancy between Siggy of part one and the writer of the "pre-history" in part two. Siggy of the opening section is intended simply as an eccentric and freedom-loving comic character. But the Siggy of part two appears to be a quite transparent substitute for John Irving; there is little actual connection between him and the character we have seen absurdly stealing salt shakers and generally acting out an immature version of human freedom. The first Siggy is both pompous and ludicrous; his "poetry" and axioms (frequently quoted by Hannes) are largely clumsy or silly or obvious or all three. The second Siggy possesses genuine irony and has come not only to understand the complicated dynamics of Austrian-Yugoslavian history, but movingly to evoke them. After this witness, it is hard to imagine his indulgence in such pure silliness as we find in part one. Given their attitudes, even as a symbolic act the zoo bust must fail; Siggy and Hannes lend it more nearly the tone of a fraternity lark than an act of ritual defiance. We would expect that the young man who had traced his family through the trauma of World War II, who had become the sole survivor of that family (thus making him representative of the lives disrupted by that upheaval), who has developed an historical vision, would recognize the trivialization involved in their activities.

There are, therefore, really two novels as well as two Siggys in Irving's book. Siggy's bizarre, sudden and needless death abruptly halts the "road" novel with its frequent cuteness of both style and substance and introduces the Siggy of the journals—or, to be more precise, the Siggy of the "pre-history," since the zoo bust largely reflects the tone and atmosphere of part one. Hannes is changed less radically in this shift; he seems to be forced by the novelist to bear the burden of both the comic saga of youthful free spirits *and* the altogether more interesting perspective that emerges from the journals. The Hannes of part three is a somewhat more interesting character. It might be argued that, with Siggy gone—for whose death Hannes feels some vague guilt—he is even more than before Siggy's alter ego, forced to assume his crazy task. While this is true, it is also the case that Hannes is deeply affected by that guilt and required to act on his own. The impact on his character is obvious; less and less secure he gradually loses self-control, even as he speculates on the significance of his actions in a way he never could have done while Siggy was alive. But having said this, we need to acknowledge that the figure who emerges is neither coherent nor well-developed, and we must observe that his change more nearly reflects Irving's new interests in the world he comes to envision in part two than the organic growth and development inherent in Hannes's character as it is initially portrayed.

That world is the uncertain prototype of the world according to Irving, a place where, as Marilyn French says, we are constantly aware of "the terrifying contingency of human life" and in which "the great equalizer is death and its harbinger, accident."[3] In fact there is no genuine preparation for Siggy's early death (though in retrospect we recognize a few ironic hints) and its violent intrusion is characteristic of all of Irving's fiction but without his usual logic. An entry in Siggy's zoo watch notebook is interesting in this regard:

> At the risk of sounding polemical, I'd like to say that there are two ways to live a long time in this world. One is to trade with violence strictly as a free agent, with no cause or love that overlaps what's expedient; and if you give no direct answers, you'll never be discovered as lying to protect yourself. But I don't exactly know what the other way to live a long time is, although I believe it involves incredible luck. There certainly is another way, though, because it's not *always* the O. Schrutts who live a long time. There are just a few survivors of a different nature around.
> I think that patience has something to do with it too. (242)

The last sentence refers, of course, to old Watzek-Trummer, who, however battered, is the novel's only true survivor—physically as well as emotionally and intellectually. But the world possesses few Watzek-Trummers (as the vagueness of the "other way" suggests). At any rate, Irving will show us the eventual ending of nearly everybody in *Garp* and *The Hotel New Hampshire*. As for trading "with violence as a free agent," if Vratno's example means anything, it suggests that remaining uncommitted does not guarantee longevity.

The "gale of the world" refrain in *Setting Free the Bears*[4]—the first of several such expressions of the "terrifying contingency" in Irving's fiction, other examples being the ever-present "Undertoad" in *Garp* and the "keep passing the open windows" of *The Hotel New Hampshire*—is used initially by Colonel Drazha Mihailovich, the Chetnik leader whose patriotism and fierce courage lead eventually to his execution by the very Yugoslavians for whom he had fought. Siggy calls Mihailovich "the last honest and stupid liberator or revolutionary left in the world" (233), stupid, perhaps, because as Wut points out, he is utterly innocent of the propaganda so successfully employed by Tito's communists. Siggy's description is ironic; he himself, the spiritual heir of the radically idealistic Zahn Glanz, is really the novel's last stupid liberator (Hannes has other motives) and his stupidity represents a failure to reckon with the "contingency." Mihailovich reaches his highest point of understanding at his trial: "I wanted much . . . I started much . . . but the gale of the world blew away me and my work" (265). The simple dignity and stark pathos of this statement underscore the fact that his stupidity is more nearly radical innocence concerning the nature of things than weakness of intellect. Speaking of the failure of an earlier zoo liberator (this episode in Viennese history fascinates Irving and he will return to it in several of his novels), Siggy says "and so his good intentions backfired" (218), though the failure "is little-known history now" (217). Again the irony: this is "history" that the modern would-be liberator should have absorbed. More like the Chetnik or Zahn Glanz than like Tito, Siggy fails to learn essential lessons about the world in time.

The implication is not necessarily, however, that acquiescence is the only appropriate response to the gale. The character of Vratno is carefully constructed to illustrate the ironies of the noncommitted; the custardlike ending of that sly survivor indicates that he was, finally, not so sly after all. But Irving, forced to modify his comic novel by adding a dimension that his vigorous imagination cannot deny, offers us no successful model—unless it is Watzek-Trummer—and communicates his own ambivalence not only through the fate of most of the major characters but also in his portrayal of Austria's pre-*Anschluss* dilemma, as personified in Chancellor Schuschnigg. On one hand Irving seems to condemn the last pre-Hitler chancellor of Austria—he steps backward again and again as patriots like Siggy's grandfather rage—but, on the other hand, he clearly sympathizes with Schuschnigg's insoluble problem; Austria faces submission, or a bloodbath and then submission. As Irving's awareness of the "terrifying contingency" grows, he will more and more come to see how he can use the comic vision as a means of serious confrontation with a world that faces such dilemmas. Garp will learn how to live and die with grace, utterly aware of, yet not willing to acquiesce to, the gale. But here Irving's unsureness results in an unsure novel, though one that, after its lightweight beginning, goes on at least to acknowledge the existential realities of modern life.

"Literary Reasons"

Seen in the past, the gale of the world takes the form of history and Grandfather Marter, Watzek-Trummer, and Siggy all are historians of varying degrees of understanding. Whatever his failings of comprehension, history dominates Siggy's sense of himself and his world. His first journal entry in Hannes's selection is preoccupied with the Second World War (and he notes Hannes's noninvolvement in that epoch) and with the way in which history—or in a sense for his generation the absence of history—impinges on life:

I was in the right place for the war, all right, but it passed me by when I was in the womb, and on my way there—and again too fresh from the womb to even take part in the post-mortem. That's a bit of what you live with if you're twenty-one in 1967, in Austria; you don't have a history, really, and no immediate future that you can see. What I mean is, we're at an interim age in an interim time, we're alive between two times of monstrous decisions—one past, the other coming. We're taking up the lag in history, for who knows how long. (104)

As a result, Siggy feels himself to have had only a "pre-history—a womb and pre-womb existence at a time when great popular decisions with terrible consequences were being made" (104). He fears that he "may be fifty" before such events happen again and he contrasts the situation in Austria with the political activism of the civil rights era in America. The zoo bust will, therefore, be a way of making history—symbolically—and at the same time commenting on the past in an Austria personified by its capital. Vienna is "all pre-history— smug and secretive. It leaves me out, every time. But if we're supposed to be the generation that's to profit from our elders' mistakes, I feel I ought to know everyone's error" (105). But is this a problem only in Austria and Europe? In a moment during which the ventriloquism of this novel is most obvious, Irving has Siggy acknowledge that "*anyone* has a pre-history. Feeling that you live at an interim time is something in the nature of being born and all the things that never happen to you after birth" (105). It is, therefore, actually no different in America; growing up brings an awareness of a past that you can never affect and a future you feel unable to shape. Almost everyone everywhere and at all times lives in an interim age; action appears to be significant only in retrospect and the future is too far away to anticipate.

Such a realization raises questions about one's ability to make sense out of history—the gale as recorded event. If the "terrifying contingency of human life" reluctantly evoked in *Bears* offers one major sign of Irving's future preoccupations, then the second is his concern with art-as-order, a concern that will reappear in different forms in each subsequent novel. History as a true discipline is both art and its metaphor; the historian interprets by giving shape to a sequence of events, not by merely recording those events. If Siggy is his parents' historian, then Hannes is Siggy's. Recovering from his own bee stings and deeply shocked by Siggy's death into a new awareness of Siggy's past, their relationship, and his own character, Hannes pores over his friend's journals. Temporarily immobilized physically and, in a sense, mentally, like any historian—or artist—he tries to make sense out of Siggy's chaotic legacy. As it happens, Hannes's imagination is not sufficient to the task; Irving has not prepared him for this role—there is too little substance. About Siggy's two very different journals he concludes, for example, that "certainly Siggy made some obscure connections between his awesome history and his scheme for busting the zoo; though, for my own part, I can't speak too well for the logic in that" (263). This conclusion is, of course, shallow and absurd; we have seen how closely related are the two journals. But Hannes does have a vague compulsion to shape these materials "if only," he says in a marvelously ironic observation, "for literary reasons." By "literary reasons" he *thinks* he means the length, chaotic condition, and quality of Siggy's writings; the "if only" perfectly completes the reductive context in which art is mentioned. Yet his "idea to interleaf" the journals reflects a real, if primitive, desire for aesthetic order; the confusion of the immediate past followed by the turbulence of the journals demands that he make some sense out of Siggy's—and now his—world.

However limited Hannes may be, he is the first of a number of artist figures that Irving dramatizes who seek what, for much of the modern world, seems to be the only remaining form of order and therefore significance that remains. In Michael Priestley's words, "as a person, neither [Hannes] Graff nor Siggy had any control over the greater powers that imposed order upon the world of Vienna; but as the narrator, Graff tries to impose his order on a fictional world that he has created by telling the story."[5]

As a narrator, Hannes leaves much to be desired. Apparently intended to be naive (as the above quotation suggests) he is more nearly opaque; we see clearly neither through nor around him. But viewed as a narrational device, it is not too farfetched to see how his intended, if not realized, function in the novel could eventually lead to the narrative voice of *Garp,* which brilliantly illuminates the experience of that novel in a way that a first-person narrator would have been unable to do. It is a considerble distance from this first hesitant experimentation with narration to the consummate mastery of point of view in the later novel, but in his next book, *The Water-Method Man,* Irving will move in that direction.

Chapter Three
The Water-Method Man:
From Autobiography to Art

Setting Free the Bears appears to have been initially intended as a comic novel in the traditional picaresque mode. It was to have been traditional, too, in its comic significance: the victory of youth, vitality, life. Long before the book's end, but especially in the climactic zoo bust, however, the positive nature of traditional comedy is lost or at least severely diminished. Beyond questions concerning Irving's artistic maturity (*Bears* clearly suffers common problems of a first novel), the work suggests the writer's deep ambivalence toward his materials, at least toward Siggy's compelling and dual history and the implications for modern experience inherent in that history. The zoo bust—which might have been treated simply as a sustained comic experience, the humor of which would have emerged from its utter absurdity and its harmlessly chaotic consequences—turns instead into a nightmare, and the planned "liberation" produces only victims. Such a conclusion, which Irving seemingly wishes to mute in the novel's last pages, follows the tragic logic of Siggy's past; his "pre-history" is Europe's history and the zoo bust but a metaphor for its disastrous outcome.

The thoughtful reader of *Bears* may therefore have understandably concluded that Irving was about to take his place, perhaps unwillingly, among the Barths and the Pynchons of modern fiction—comedy darkening into black humor, hope turning to despair—but he would have been wrong. Nothing is more characteristic of Irving's ambivalence and therefore his undulating line of development than the shift between *Bears* and his second novel, *The Water-Method Man* (or, for that matter, the subsequent shift between that novel and his third, *The 158-Pound Marriage*). Looking back in 1979 from the perspective of *The World According to Garp,* published in the previous year, Irving admitted that in *Water-Method Man* he had "wanted to write a book, if I could, with a happy ending, because I didn't feel I had a happy ending in me, and I wanted to get one. I wanted to write a book that was absolutely comic."[1] That desire—the driving force behind not only *Water-Method Man* but also *Garp* and some aspects of *The Hotel New Hampshire* as well—was based not simply on literary strategy, though that clearly played its part, but also on an emerging vision of the world that, while fully aware of its sources, was hostile to contemporary despair.

In *Daniel Martin*, the English novelist John Fowles has his playwright protagonist come eventually to reject "a received idea of the [modern] age . . . that only a tragic, absurdist, black-comic view . . . of human destiny could be counted as truly representative and 'serious.' " Martin vigorously repudiates what is usually called postmodernism: "to hell with cultural fashion; to hell with elitist guilt; to hell with existentialist nausea," and the rejection appears to be Fowles's as well.[2] As Eleanor Wymard has pointed out in calling attention to these comments by Martin, for all their differences, Fowles and Irving share "the generous perspective of the comic vision."[3] By the time of *Garp*, Irving will be ready to make his novelist hero argue for the "serious" nature of comedy (for example, in Garp's debate with the lady from Findlay, Ohio). In that novel he will dramatize a comic-tragic vision of a life, a perspective already latent in *Bears* and one that seems to pervade all his later fiction. One must recognize that "the world *is* out of control," he will later argue, and that humor and sadness are our "consolation."[4] *The Water-Method Man*, however, is a purer, more overt embodiment of the traditionally positive mode and, except for aspects of the fictional "Old Low Norse" poem that its protagonist translates, the book's humor is little darkened by the ever-present dangers and cruelties of life characteristic of the other novels.

"A Narrow, Winding Road"

The delightful comedy *Water-Method Man* is an enormous improvement over the earlier *Bears*. In every respect—especially in the creation of strong characters and in the control of tone—the work marks a considerable maturation of Irving's talent. And while the novel lacks the massive quality of *Garp* or the dream dimension of *Hotel New Hampshire* or the serious "polemic" of *Cider House*, it yet remains Irving's most complex novel in terms of narrative technique. Both the continual manipulation of point of view and dramatic and frequent shifts in the novel's time sequence complicate an otherwise relatively straightforward plot.

The story opens in the New York office of a noted French urologist to whom Fred "Bogus" Trumper has gone for help with a long-standing difficulty: both urination and sexual climax cause him much pain. At the moment he is living with Tulpen; like her he works for an independent filmmaker, Ralph Packer, as a sound engineer. With Tulpen he has a "new life" and therefore wants it "to change" accordingly. The novel will move forward from this point, but much of what follows will also take him back into his past—recent and distant. The doctor recommends an operation (examination has shown that Trumper's "urinary tract is a narrow and winding road") but for the moment Trumper rejects remedial surgery in favor of "the water-method"—large quantities of water to be drunk before and after sex intended to wash away the offending germs that lodge in the irregularities of his plumbing.

We will eventually discover that Trumper has come to this point by way of several sojourns in Austria as a student (often in the company of an alter ego known as Merrill Overturf), marriage to Sue "Biggie" Kunft (a member of the United States ski team), the fathering of a son, Colm, graduate school in Iowa, and the subsequent failure of his marriage and resultant flight to Vienna where, in the winter of 1969–70, he had suffered a nervous collapse. Having arrived back in New York (at the insistence of United States Treasury agents who had forced him to assist them in a drug bust), Trumper found work in Ralph Packer's film studio and a stabilizing relationship with Tulpen, a young woman whose maturity and self-control helped to compensate for his own lack of these qualities. The book's opening scene occurs when Tulpen attempts to help Trumper reorganize his chaotic life. Trumper has worked on several of Packer's avant-garde films (they had first met as students at Iowa) but when the producer makes "Fucking Up"—the story of Trumper's own tangled and irresolute existence—he once again flees, this time not to Austria but back to Iowa to finish his suspended doctoral dissertation in comparative literature, a translation of the only extant "Old Low Norse" epic, "Akthelt and Gunnel."

Trumper's real reason for leaving Tulpen and Packer is not, primarily, the embarrassing film of his own life, but rather Tulpen's desire to have a child. Despite his own hope for "a new life," he continues to suffer from a long-time ailment: entrenched immaturity and the accompanying inability to accept responsibility. He uses Tulpen's imagined infidelity with Ralph while Trumper is at last in the hospital for his remedial surgery as an excuse to escape yet another obligation. But returning to New York after completing his translation and receiving his degree, Trumper sees "Fucking Up" and is forced to acknowledge Tulpen's innocence. He also discovers himself to be a father again, Tulpen having given birth to a baby boy in his absence. He is accepted back into the household by Tulpen and into the studio by Ralph.

Having long since come to accept Biggie's remarriage to his own best friend, Couth (a tranquil photographer and caretaker of a large sea-side estate in Maine), Trumper joins all the novel's major characters for a late fall visit to the estate in order to celebrate "Throgsgafen Day," an Old Low Norse version of American Thanksgiving. Couth and Biggie have also just had a child, Ralph Packer's new wife is expecting a baby, and Trumper and Tulpen bring their infant Merrill. Thus the novel concludes not only with Trumper's reentry into a life of responsibility and human commitment, but also with a general reconciliation and a celebration of marriage and childbirth—in terms of the comic vision, of life itself.

"How Is Anything Related to Anything Else?"

In *Bears* Irving had experimented with point of view to the extent that he had interpolated Siggy's first-person journals and histories into Hannes's first person narrative, and with time insofar as he had moved back and forth between the present narrative and the past of Siggy's histories. In *Water-Method Man* he experiments much more extensively, creating a complex narrative pattern and a several-layered time scheme, which are largely successful in dramatizing the nature of Trumper's mind and experience.

Roughly speaking, the initial third of the novel alternates between first and third person, the middle section employs mostly third person, and the final third is mixed, some chapters employing both forms. In addition, three early chapters are epistolary. The effect achieved is that of a continual refocusing of dual lenses, the first person clearly solipsistic and the third person more objective. This distinction is not destroyed by ultimately discovering what we early suspect, that both voices are actually Trumper's; whether obviously inside or only apparently outside his mind, we recognize that (as is always the case with point of view) vantage point is crucial. This "autobiography" makes use of more than one device to create a sense of its author's consciousness; it provides a refraction of perspective that allows us to feel the tension between fact and feeling, experience and the impression it leaves.

Just as point of view fluctuates continuously in the novel, so the time scheme alternates between the present and several periods in the past. The novel's present occurs in the months following the spring of 1970; it begins with Trumper's life in New York, follows his return to Iowa, and concludes with his return to New York. The past, narrated in separate chapters interspersed throughout the book, takes place largely at the University of Iowa in the fall of 1969 during the collapse of Trumper's marriage to Biggie, and in Vienna in the winter and spring of 1969–70 where, searching for his almost mythical friend Merrill Overturf, he suffers a nervous breakdown. But other past times emerge, too, primarily his youth in New England and one of several trips to Austria—the occasion on which he meets Biggie and sees Merrill for the last time. Very much as the multiple points of view allow us several perspectives on Trumper's character, so these juxtaposed periods of his life offer us simultaneously cause and effect; Trumper's funny-sad attempts at self-control and self-knowledge are located not in some vague, reported past, but always in the living present. While at some points manipulation of point of view may seem merely whimsical, the interleafing of time seems fully functional and justified. This process is especially effective regarding the critical parallel between his relationships with Biggie and Tulpen; here we see both repetition and significant change, as does Trumper himself.

As the reader of *Garp* knows, like other modern writers Irving has his aesthetically self-reflective (and self-reflexive) moments. Chapter 27 of *Water-Method Man*—"How Is Anything Related to Anything Else?"—calls attention to the importance of the ordering and interpreting function of verbal art—to writing as self-therapy. But first Irving introduces a satirical discussion of the fictitious postmodernist writer Helmbart, whose novel *Vital Telegrams* has fascinated Ralph Packer and, in some vague way, influenced his filmmaking style. "The structure is everything," Ralph argues: "Then he quoted a blurb from the book jacket which said that Helmbart had achieved some kind of breakthrough. 'The transitions—all the associations, in fact— are syntactical, rhetorical, *structural*; it is almost a story of sentence structure rather than of characters; Helmbart complicates variations on forms of sentences rather than plot,' it read" (259). Presumably in a truly modern, absurdist view there can be none of the connections about which the chapter's title asks, hence no conventional plot. But no one, including Ralph, actually *likes* the book and, using a device that he will rely on extensively in *Garp,* Irving then includes chapter 77 of Helmbart's novel, a piece of writing that makes even less sense than the blurb writer's pretentious jargon. The source of humor here is clear; like other modern writers Irving has rejected doctrinaire realism, but he does not share the avant-garde's classic obsession with the artist's medium—whether with structure or language—and strong characters along with the action they produce remain central to his fiction. However reflexive, his ongoing concern is hardly Barthian (even in *Garp* where the protagonist is specifically a writer concerned, even obsessed, with the creative act), since in Barth that concern seems all too often to be the center of the fiction, where in Irving it only helps to define the center.

For all of his ordinariness Trumper is, however, that most ubiquitous of modern characters—an artist figure. In *Bears* Irving had toyed with the creative sensibility in Hannes, but that character is as unsuccessful as an artist as he is in most other respects. Trumper, on the other hand, quite naturally displays his creative tendencies as he gropes toward self-understanding. The uses to which he puts his tape recorder, his creative "translation" of "Akthelt and Gunnel" and his subsequent screenplay based on the poem—even his instinctive purchase of a typewriter as he arrives to hide his disintegrating life in a bordello-cum-pension in Vienna—all dramatize his artistic nature. Chapter 27 shows Trumper moving from his bafflement at Ralph's admiration for *Vital Telegrams* to his own genuine need to explain his life by writing about it ("Jesus, I shall keep a diary, Trumper thought" [263]). As in all verbal art "questions were raised" and "analogies leaped to his mind" (264), but at first nothing would come. Finally,

> He did manage a sentence. It didn't seem to be a diary sort of sentence; in fact, it was a real cliff-hanger of an opening line. But he wrote it in spite of himself:
> "Her gynecologist recommended him to me."
> What a way to begin a diary! The question struck him: How is anything related to anything else? But he had to begin somewhere. (265)

The autobiographical nature of his writing emphasizes the fact that he is not "a man speaking to men" but rather a modern artist who would share with others that which he has been able to say to himself. It is not simply that to "know thyself" remains the central injunction of Western culture—and is endlessly reiterated in the popular slogans of the counterculture in which Trumper lives—but that to know thyself by creating in its entirety one's reality is the only mode for the existential writer to adopt.

Trumper's Change

When the novel begins Trumper wants "to change"—his twisted life as much as his crooked urinary tract—and it remains for the novel to show from what to what. A simple operation would solve his physical problem as would, it appears to the outsider, a simple acceptance of reality-as-it-is solve his emotional problems. But Trumper is a confirmed evader; insecurity and doubt have combined to produce a self-proclaimed liar (whose earliest nickname is Bogus), a failure in his own eyes who has left his wife, dropped out of graduate school (in *Bears,* Siggy and Hannes had also both abandoned the university), and suffered a nervous collapse. But he has not so much lied to himself—or even to the world, for that matter—as he has avoided coming to grips with his own nature as the source of his problems. Trumper has never fully grown up, hence maturation and self-knowledge—neither possible without the other—are the main themes of this novel.

After the crucial breakup of his marriage to Biggie, Trumper's self-distrust and intensified caution lead to his increased evasion of self-knowledge. Since he is the book's narrator, the inattentive reader—like other characters in the novel—may conclude that evasion merely disguises the fact that he has *no* self—no real center. In Ralph Packer's film about Trumper's life, one reviewer complains that we "never get to the bottom of what makes the main character tick" (359) and Ralph himself insists that in actual life Trumper doesn't "come across" (93). In her anger and frustration at Trumper's refusal to have a baby, Tulpen is inclined to go one step farther than Ralph:

> "No one knows you, Trumper! You don't *convey* anything. You don't do much, either. Things just sort of happen to you, and they don't even add up to anything. You don't make anything of what happens to you. Ralph

says you must be very complicated, Trumper. He thinks you must have a
mysterious core under the surface."

Trumper stared into the fish tank. *Where is the talking eel?*

"And what do *you* think, Tulpen?" he asked her. "What do you think's
under the surface?"

"Another surface," she said, and he stared at her. "Or maybe just that
one surface," she said, "with nothing under it." (94)

Her indictment bears a striking likeness to a passage in John Barth's
second novel, the nihilistic comedy *The End of the Road*. Rennie, a
married women, confronts her lover, Jake Horner: "You know what
I've come to think, Jake? I think you don't exist at all. There's too
many of you. It's more than just masks that you put on and take
off—we all have masks. But you're different all the way through, every time. You cancel yourself out. You're more like somebody in a
dream. You're not strong and you're not weak. You're nothing."
(67). Horner is, in fact, what Rennie claims; his first-person narrative
opens with "in a sense, I am Jacob Horner," and goes on to portray
a character who is all "surface."

But Tulpen does, finally, know who Trumper is, and the reader
comes to recognize that he is neither mysteriously complex nor simply
"bogus" but, rather, inaccessible until he has first become accessible
to *himself.* His life and his penis have a kink or two in them and the
book is the story of how he comes to straighten them both out—the
former amusingly symbolized by the latter. When all is said and
done, Irving's story concerns itself with the ordinary agonies of contemporary life, and our pleasure lies in its very unpretentiousness.
Barth's *End of the Road,* on the other hand, is a terrifying novel of
ideas, terrifying because, for all its hard-edged humor, it is built on
assumptions that are themselves frightening.

Unlike Helmbart, then, Irving starts with character, not "structure"; unlike Barth he does not place theme above the action produced as that character takes his place in life. He does not develop a
thesis but rather explores a specific condition—hence the fuzzy edges,
the slightly blurred focus, the missing crispness of abstract principle
when contrasted with Barth.

When Trumper, the son of a urologist and a long sufferer, diagno-
ses his own urinary ailment as "nonspecific," Dr. Vigneron, his
French specialist, points out that nothing could be much more
specific than a birth defect that leaves one's urinary tract " a narrow,

winding road." As Ruppersburg has pointed out, Trumper's difficulty
is an apt "metaphor for his own life. . . . Urination and sex are necessary functions of life" and Trumper "can have neither without serious pain, which warps his attitude toward love and life in general."[5]
The symbolism is clear: Trumper has been able to accept neither the
truth of his own body nor its metaphorical significance to his life. But
he eventually gropes his way down that narrow, winding road and the
journey becomes a comic quest for the self-knowledge and self-accep-
tance necessary to make life and love—hence marriage and parenthood—possible.

Trumper is twenty-eight-years-old in 1970, the time at which the
story is told. While the novel's sociology belongs to the sixties
(Kent's day-glow orange shirt, the hippie commune documented in
one of Ralph Packer's films) and while there is an identifiable ambience (Iowa graduate school, the community of avant-garde filmmakers
in Greenwich Village) Irving mentions few specific dates; more important, actual events such as the Vietnam war or real people of that
chaotic period are carefully avoided. Trumper could be said to suffer
the dislocations and insecurities of an anxious age, yet he is no exem-
plar. And however unheroic, he is no antihero in the pattern of
Barth's Jake Horner, that outrider for the postmodernist vanguard.
Terribly ordinary, he is yet fully himself, a character adrift in his *own*
time and place, bumbling in his own vulnerable way toward some yet
hopeful solution he cannot guess, preoccupied with a more broadly
modern quest for self-realization. Horner, on the other hand, has
been morally, even psychologically, lobotomized; he merely hopes to
avoid literal paralysis. In this regard, as in several others, Trumper
has more in common with the young men of Sherwood Anderson than
he does with the protagonists of Barth, whereas Barth's Horner may
be a logical extension of Hemingway's psychologically wounded Nick
Adams.

Like Siggy and Hannes, Trumper at present has "no plans" (89).
For different reasons and to a less radical extent, he is in danger of
suffering the paralysis that finally claims Jake Horner. Short of simply
reacting to the unruly events of his life (e.g., he twice runs away from
relationships he cannot handle), he finds for a while no course of action that offers more hope than any other. A keen observer of his own
nature and not slow to confess his many inadequacies, at least to himself, Trumper is nonetheless at a loss as to what to make of his life—
or do with himself. His dilemma concerns how to understand himself

and yet not fall into a solipsistic trap, how to become necessarily self-
aware and yet not be, as one reviewer of Packer's film" Fucking Up"
calls him, "an absolute paranoiac victimized by his own self-analysis"
(359).

Eventually such self-realization must come, and its result must be,
the novel suggests, a realization of his own emotional immaturity.
Most of the book's other characters—especially the women—are already "adults" (Tulpen has, for example, "outgrown having to talk
about herself" [18] and Biggie, though she may still dream of the
giant slalom, attempts to face and solve their domestic problems).
Even that enfant terrible of the film world, Ralph Packer, commits
himself to marriage and profession. But Trumper unconsciously fights
a rearguard action against maturity and, though he leans on his best
friend from childhood (the dependable Couth who takes over his marriage for him), Trumper yearns to associate again with Merrill Overturf, the zany and madly reckless diabetic whom Trumper had met
in Austria and whose expatriate wanderings (the very model of male
freedom) end in death before Trumper can once again locate him.
When Trumper flees his marriage after events that, if not wholly his
fault yet result from his own refusal to face reality, he instinctively
returns to Vienna to find the elusive Merrill, who has actually
drowned in a quixotic attempt to locate a Nazi tank sunk in the Dan-
ube. Merrill's tank search equates with Siggy's zoo bust, but Merrill
is a less imposing character and, at any rate, by the time Trumper
learns of Merrill's death his own life is too shattered to pick up and
complete his friend's quest, as Hannes, whose unjustified sense of betrayal and guilt drove him to the very end, had completed Siggy's zoo
liberation. In *Bears* the figure of a strong sane women capable of opposing male absurdity has not yet emerged. Hannes is utterly domi-
nated by Siggy and, even after his friend's death, Gallen (who will be
developed in Biggie, Tulpen, and later Irving women) remains unable
to save him from that negative influence.

Trumper's "longest dreams are about heroes. Accordingly, he
dreams of Merrill Overturf" (219). Merrill had, in fact, been the
"great illusion" of Trumper's illusion-filled life (127), an influence
nearly strong enough to cause him to lose Biggie at the moment when
he first found her. He was, moreover, the partial cause of Trumper's
final separation from a woman whose bigness is certainly more, Irving
makes clear, than physical. Irving's attitude toward Biggie appears

somewhat ambivalent, but he seems finally to emphasize not her earth-mother role so much as her emotional maturity and sense of responsibility. Just before Trumper's escape from Iowa, he and Biggie had quarreled over Merrill, Biggie rightly accusing Merrill of childishness and adolescent escapism, while Trumper insists on his courage.

It is not, however, Merrill's courage but rather his freedom that attracts Trumper at this juncture. But he must come, if only subconsciously, to recognize that Merrill's kind of freedom was a form of cowardice or—at best—selfishness. Merrill had been initially put off by the realization that Trumper and Biggie were genuinely in love, that what they wanted was a permanent relationship: "You're not any fun to be with. . . .You're in love, you know. . . .I don't want anything to do with either of you" (138). Later, when after Colm's birth Trumper had tried to explain to Merrill how "children give you a sudden sense of your own mortality" (157), he had failed; neither mortality nor children are allowed to enter Merrill's narcissistic consciousness—yet neither is ever far from Trumper's. Merrill, who represents that part of Trumper that denies life and therefore cannot grow, must be killed off so that Trumper can finally transcend his own adolescent, escapist tendencies.

In *The Water-Method Man* then, Irving continues his study of the protagonist's emotional development in the context of sexual, familial, and social relationships. Trumper must come to accept himself before he can finally accept others—a lesson Hannes appears to be still unwilling to learn at the end of *Bears* but which, in some provisional way, Trumper does come to accept: roughly speaking, he starts where Hannes leaves off. At the novel's conclusion he finally arrives, in one sense, at the beginning—of his book and of the "new life" he had claimed to desire in chapter one. Then, however, he had chosen the water-method rather than undergo a small but necessary and painful (necessary *because* painful?) operation, a latter day puberty rite of sorts. By the novel's conclusion he has had the surgery, finished his dissertation and degree, reconciled himself with his father, accepted the loss of Biggie and Colm, and embraced the love of Tulpen and her baby.

"What have I begun? he wonders" as near the end of the book he starts the novel that we have all along been reading. Both penile and, presumably, mental blocks have been removed, and he is ready to emerge as some kind of an artist (novelist? screenwriter?) but not because Irving has designed the novel so as to suggest some clear in-

sight, some "statement" to which Trumper's life will "add up." This
conclusion, and new starting point, is encouraging but vague:

> What have I begun? he wondered. He didn't know. He put the paper
> with these crude beginnings in his pocket to save for a time when he had
> more to say.
> He wished he understood what made him feel so restless. Then it occurred
> to him that he was actually at peace with himself for the first time in his
> life. He realized how much he'd been anticipating peace someday, but the
> feeling was not what he'd expected. He used to think that peace was a state
> he would achieve, but the peace he was feeling was like a force he'd submit-
> ted to. God, why should peace depress me? he thought. But he wasn't de-
> pressed, exactly. Nothing was exact. (377)

For all its wild comedy, the ending of *Bears* suggests a barely veiled
hopelessness; the chaos of the zoo bust, when it finally comes, reflects
the unresolved confusion of Hannes's mind, as well as the unreconciled violence of Europe's recent past—Hannes is still "on the road."
Water-Method Man, however, ends in peace and reconciliation, and
that ending helps chart the directions Irving's imagination will take
in his last three novels, *Garp, Hotel New Hampshire,* and *Cider House,*
however more difficult that process will become.

The Comic Vision

If there is no existential despair in *Water-Method Man* and hence no
sardonic humor, neither is there any firmly based victory over "the
world"—none, that is, beyond the inescapable victory in comedy itself which Irving claimed to have literally willed into existence here.
Whatever its source, "the peace" Trumper feels represents the completion of comedy's archetypal pattern, the movement from difficulty
and pain to success and happiness.

In *Bears* Irving had demonstrated his skill in constructing extended, comic scenes; for instance, Siggy's naked attack on the
drunken milkman is excellent. But pehaps the most powerful scene
in the novel—Siggy's and Hannes's freewheeling descent from the
mountain on a runaway motorcycle—ends in a genuine disaster
which, while retaining its comic-strip madness, results in the bee and
honeycoated death of Siggy beneath the wagon load of hives. The humor remains but its source shifts; the same can be said of Wut's awful

death in the latrine and even of the zoo bust itself. In *Water-Method Man,* however, such scenes—aside from significant exceptions in "Akthelt and Gunnel"—for the most part retain a less sinister comic purity. A number could be cited: Trumper's cornfield seduction of (or by) Lydia Kindle and its wonderfully extended aftermath, his souvenir-board defeat at the Iowa-Notre Dame game, his initiation into skiing under Merrill's guidance, Biggie's interview on Austrian TV, Trumper in the waiting room of his urologist, and his fantasy of the dead patron in a Viennese brothel. Of these scenes, the first—the encounter of bearish Trumper with Lydia Kindle and its duck hunting sequel—is clearly the most successful and represents the qualities that Irving's very considerable talent for this sort of thing produces: enormous verve, excitement, zany excess, funny pathos. Such scenes, largely missing from his next novel, *The 158-Pound Marriage,* return to become the glory of *Garp.*

Well-drawn comic characters emerge, too. Besides the wonderful Trumper himself there is Ralph, Kent, Merrill—even old Fitch, the obsessive Iowa lawn-raker and keeper of noctural confidences. Trumper's father, the cranky and exceedingly illiberal New Hampshire urologist, represents the antagonist of traditional comedy; he is the voice of restraint, custom, conventional social and professional judgment, the eternal parent. But Dr. Trumper is only a residual element of the older comic mode.

Trumper himself, as we have seen, is his own antagonist; his quirks, psychic distortions, and failings impede his development. He not only survives Dr. Trumper and all that he stands for, but he also overcomes the inadequacies of self; in so doing he embodies the "self-preservation, self-restraint, functional tendency" that Susanne Langer sees as central to the comic hero.[6] *Bears* had, perhaps unintentionally, dramatized the failures of human development and the resultant failure of human commitment. In *Water-Method Man* Irving continues his examination of these problems, but shifts the focus to more important relationships. Trumper has in the past, failed to develop and, therefore, also failed as husband and father. But having come through the hell of his Vienna breakdown and his ensuing self-discovery through art, Trumper commits himself in a way Hannes clearly cannot.

Hence the novel ends on a note more profoundly comic than that produced by the laughter itself. At the heart of the traditional comic vision that Irving embraces in this novel is a sense of affirmation, not so much of conventional morality as of life itself. The symbol of that positive view is marriage, which reconstitutes society and joins sexual desire with renewal through childbirth—it is the concrete embodiment of a victory of youth over age, life over those forces that would deny it. Appropriately—thematically as well as structurally—Irving concludes *Water-Method Man* with a "Throgsgafen Day" celebration at the Pillsbury estate, an occasion that joins the sacramental intentions of the Pilgrims with a fully pagan "Old Low Norse" appreciation of earthly pleasures. Trumper creates this occasion with his translation of "Akthelt and Gunnel," but in the novel the event represents his own renewal and his reintegration into his society. Irving brings the book's main participants back on stage one more time: Biggie, Couth, Colm, and Colm's new sibling; Ralph and his very pregnant bride Matje; Trumper, Tulpen, and their new baby Merrill. Then, on the novel's last page, all of these characters appear in various windows and doors of the great old mansion to shout their Throgsgafen Day morning greetings to each other and especially to salute a delighted Trumper, who appears before the house. Northrop Frye's description of a comic finale bears an uncanny likeness to the entire event: "In the last scene, when the dramatist usually tries to get all his characters on the stage at once, the audience witnesses the birth of a renewed sense of social integration. In comedy as in life the regular expression of this is a festival, whether a marriage, a dance, or a feast."[7] "The great houseful of flesh," of husbands, wives, and babies, hums with the preparation for a huge feast in celebration of reconciliation and human continuity.

Having earlier been reconciled with his father, Trumper has also rejoined Ralph and they have begun a more ambitious film project. Biggie, in her love for Couth and her continuing affection for Trumper, has forgiven him, and he has at last accepted both losing her and the ever-widening distance between himself and Colm. Tulpen has received Trumper back into her life because, having accepted himself, he is now ready to accept their child and the permanent responsibility of marriage. Trumper is no longer "Fucking Up"; though life with its complexity is neither clear nor easy, as a successful survivor, he identifies with Moby Dick and accepts the peace for what it is worth:

Bogus wondered what he could have thought he wanted. But the kitchen was far too flurried for thinking; bodies were everywhere. So what if dog puke still lurked unseen in the laundry room! In good company we can be brave.

Mindful of his scars, his old harpoons and things, Bogus Trumper smiled cautiously at all the good flesh around him. (381)

The smile is indeed cautious but justified; reborn out of his old, distorted and retarded self, Trumper at last has changed.

Toward *158-Pound Marriage* and *The World According to Garp*

Love, sex, reproduction—the affirmation of life and the reassertion of human continuity—with this, comedy demonstrates what Helen Gardner has called the "rhythm of the life of mankind, which goes on and renews itself as the life of nature does."[8] But the comedy of Irving's novels after *Water-Method Man* will complicate this basic pattern and grow darker with a continual dramatization of what in *Bears* has been already called "the gale of the world"—that ever-present potential in human affairs for cruelty, pain, chance, violence, and death. Perhaps the most significant evidence of the purely comic mode of *Water-Method Man* is the absence of any act or event even approaching the multiple disasters of the other novels (with the exceptions of *The 158-Pound Marriage* and *Cider House,* where the absence nevertheless does not produce the same benevolent world). But though Trumper's own life is fully contained by the comic vision, the fictitious "Old Low Norse" epic, "Akthelt and Gunnel," parts of which are interpolated into the novel through direct quotation and paraphrase, offers a somewhat different perspective.

The translation of this wretched poem is Trumper's dissertation project. During his first attempt, while yet married to Biggie, he had started out to produce a faithful rendering of the original, but as the lugubrious text moved toward its painful outcome, Trumper had gradually translated it more and more freely until eventually he was inventing as much as he was translating. At stanza 280 he returned to a literal translation:

> Gunnel uppvaktat att titta Akthelt.
> Hanz kniv af slik lang.
> Uden hun kende inde hunz hjert
> Den varld af ogsa mektig.

> Gunnell loved to look at Akthelt.
> His knife was so long.
> But she knew in her heart
> The world was too strong.
>
> (32)

Even his dissertation director laughed at these dreadful lines. But Trumper stopped translating, not because of the absurd quality but because even earlier he had become uneasy. Biggie had laughed too but "*I* didn't laugh. The world *is* too strong—I saw it all coming!— The author was trying to foreshadow the inevitable doom! Clearly Akthelt and Gunnel were headed for grief. I knew, and I simply didn't want to see it out" (32–33). However, Trumper sympathizes rather than empathizes; "the world was too strong—for him! He saw *himself* headed for grief" (33). His eventual completion of an accurate, scholarly translation symbolizes (as does his willingness to undergo the urinary operation) his personal development. He must and does accept the fact that the clumsy epic, like life, "ends rather badly" (350). In *The Hotel New Hampshire* we will learn that "there are no happy endings" (168).

   Water-Method Man defies Irving's own rule; in this novel, as nowhere else in his fiction, the author insulates the sensitive hero from the violence and multiple dangers of ordinary life found in the world according to Irving. "Akthelt and Gunnel," however, details various brutalities and ends with the deaths of the good and noble lovers. In the poem, where "even sex is a blood sport" (355), neither Trumper nor the reader is fully spared. But even without the "basic pessimism" (335) and grotesquerie of the terrible saga, the world's disorder already impinges, if only in passing, on the light-hearted book. In the remarkable and ambiguous scene where he accepts the sexual favors of Lydia Kindle, Trumper is rendered sexually impotent because he sees her in a larger context: "why does my mind run to slaughter-houses, and to all the young girls raped in wars?" (179). As Gabriel Miller has rightly pointed out, the ambience here is quite close to the rape-murder scene in "The World According to Bensenhaver" chapter of *Garp*,[9] and if the final impression is comic, we are still aware of the disturbing parallel. These other uncomfortable themes will also be carried forward and developed in the following novels, especially the related issue of another group of victims, one's children.

In *Bears* there had been no marriage, let alone children. In *Water-Method Man*, however, there is a veritable explosion of childbirth as the novel moves from the selfish sexuality and emotional immaturity of Irving's first novel toward the rich complexity of love, sex, parenthood, and the awareness of mortality which will be explored so fully in *Garp* and *Hotel New Hampshire*. Already in this novel the theme of parental paranoia resulting from a sense of the radical vulnerability of children is well developed. Trumper takes Colm to the zoo because it seems to offer a safe, "controlled environment"—one need expect "no life and death struggles or failures there" (158). Ironically, however, the world of genuinely wild creatures penetrates that haven and a migrating duck, ill or wounded, crashes and dies. Colm insists on acknowledging the bird's death and consoles his father: some ducks "just get old and die, is all. Animals and birds and people" (160–61).

This scene is amusing and the humor produced by the role reversal mutes its implications. But it is touching as well; Trumper is obsessed with the realization that like the bird, his child—that epitome of innocence and vulnerability—can be maimed physically or psychically, or killed—even more easily than the rest of us. The insecurities of their existence haunts Irving like no other threat, and the nuances of that kind of significance will be greatly elaborated, especially in *Garp*.

But before he left the relatively innocent world of Trumper and started work on his most rich, Dickensian canvas, Irving would pause to focus intensely on the pleasures and complicated pain of multiple affairs in *The 158-Pound Marriage*.

Chapter Four

The 158-Pound Marriage: "A Tale by a Villain"?

The very real differences between *Setting Free the Bears* and *The Water-Method Man* are only partially explained by the processes of artistic and personal maturation that frequently occur between first and second novels. Irving was not simply developing sophisticated technical skills in his second novel; he was rapidly moving toward a clarity of vision and voice—a clarity not present in *Setting Free the Bears*. With *The Water-Method Man*, Irving explored the substantial potential of the domestic milieu for the first time and firmly established the comic mode; these characteristics have, of course, since come to define the literary universe of his mature works. And so his second novel seemed to embody the shape and form of an artistic vision firmly in the young writer's grasp.

It is somewhat peculiar, therefore, that although he appeared confident of his mode and voice in *The Water-Method Man*, Irving produced a third book whose tone, focus, and point of view are as tentative and artistically unreconciled as they had been in *Setting Free the Bears*. This ostensible regression in an otherwise powerfully developing career can perhaps be explained best by Irving's own description of that period in his life: "That's the kind of period I was in at the time: everything I read was a *labor* and it made me *angry*. It was like I lost my sense of humor."[1] The product of that very period, *The 158-Pound Marriage*, reflects something of the unpleasant state of mind Irving describes. The novel is also perhaps further explained by its imitative nature—the only book Irving has published to date that is self-consciously patterned on other novels.

Two things are immediately apparent about *The 158-Pound Marriage*: first, as he made clear, Irving was overwhelmingly indebted to and influenced by Ford Maddox Ford's *The Good Soldier* and John Hawkes's *The Blood Oranges* and consciously chose to evoke, if not parallel, both novels in his own;[2] and, second, he was, as we have seen, becoming increasingly comfortable with first person narration. The fact that both Hawkes's and Ford's novels were narrated in the first person surely enhanced Irving's imaginative attraction to these books and strengthened their artistic appeal as models for his third novel. Furthermore, one might even conjecture that since Irving was teaching at Iowa when he wrote and published *The 158-Pound Marriage* and had "lost [his] sense of humor," he was then most susceptible to external literary influences in which he was, as teacher, steeped. Unfortunately, the result of these influences is, despite his growing facility with first person narration, a not wholly satisfactory novel; it is a novel that may have suffered as much from the constrictions of its models as it was inspired by their strengths.

A Quaternion

Like its literary predecessors, *Marriage* is told in retrospect by one of the male participants—and survivors—of a ménage à trois or a ménage à quatre. In each of the three novels, the narrator apparently wishes to objectify the experience he has recently undergone; we soon discover, however, that each of the narrators is at least as intent on rationalizing his role in the affair as he is in understanding its implications. For in all three cases, the experience has led, at the very least, to temporarily destructive, if not profoundly tragic, consequences.

The basic plots of the three novels are analogous: two couples unexpectedly meet and are initially drawn together by a mixture of social circumstances, personal history, and common interests—interests that ultimately flower in comparatively hermetic environments and are transformed into sexual attractions which result in the exchange of partners.

In *Marriage*, the common experiences and interests are multiple. The narrator and Severin Winter both teach at a New England university while their wives, Utchka and Edith, are primarily occupied raising prepubescent children. Frustrated with his academic assignment as a professor of history, the narrator aspires to be an historical novelist, a fiction writer whose sensibilities are, from his perspective, clearly misplaced in the literalist world of college history teaching. Edith, too, is a writer and, as the novel unfolds, the ostensible artistic "sharing" between her and the narrator develops, as if according to a plan agreed to by all four participants, into a fully corporeal relationship, a relationship that is rather quickly replicated by the more phlegmatic Severin and Utchka.

Like the narrator, Severin has what amounts to two sometimes conflicting vocations: he teaches German at the college but is clearly more attached to his role as wrestling coach. Attracted to the physical and primal vitality that the sport so often symbolizes in Irving's work, Utchka is also drawn to Severin because they share a common ethnic heritage; albeit in very different ways, like Siggy's family in *Bears*, they both faced the horrors of the *Anschluss* in Austria, the war, and the devastating aftermath of the Allied partitioning. And while each survived (and even flourishes) as a result of that European experience, their shared language and cultural sympathy serve to create a psychic and emotional bond.

The exchange of partners, therefore, occurs in a fertile atmosphere and is accompanied by an aura of inevitability, not simply because the narrator manipulates the elements of his story so, but because the landscape is charged with Irvingesque coincidences of experience and character.

The affair moves from the experimental and tentative to the sometimes comically erotic and sophisticated to the predictably complex and messy denouement wherein Severin and Edith's marriage is restored, Utchka and her children leave the narrator for Vienna, and the narrator, puzzled and largely unenlightened by it all, decides to pursue his family and embark on the book to which he has always hoped to commit himself.

While the progress of these affairs represents the forward plot movement, the retrospective form of the novel allows the narrator not only to reveal gradually immediate past events, but to devote fairly significant portions of the narration to aspects of his own history, as well as to dwell rather extensively on the histories of the other three protagonists, a mode used in a somewhat different way by Trumper and even by Siggy in the earlier two novels. Indeed, the first three of the novel's ten chapters, while revealing some necessary details of the "quaternion" itself, are devoted primarily to the more remote histories of Utchka, Severin, and Edith, histories that symbolically and actually intersect in Vienna. From chapter 4 on, the increasingly convoluted relationships among the four are detailed, with major digressions occurring only as each character confides a portion of his or her past to lover or spouse.

The idyllic scene begins to dissolve as the inevitable complications emerge: Edith and Utchka become friends who confide in each other and even experiment sexually together; the wrestling practice room serves—as it does more powerfully in *Garp*—as an increasingly charged emotional focus for the experiences of all the major characters, as painful past and ongoing betrayals of various kinds are revealed; and finally, the children and their needs and lives quite naturally intrude on the narrow interests of their parents and introduce reality in a harsh form when the Winter girls are seriously hurt in a domestic accident, an accident that ironically precipitates the full reconciliation of the Winters' relationship and the (at least temporary) dissolution of the narrator and Utchka's marriage.

The novel ends with the narrator rather pathetically (and somewhat tentatively) resolving to pursue Utchka and the children to Vienna where they have fled, and pledging himself "to try the Bruegel book again" (254).

The Schizophrenic Vision

In terms of time, space, landscape, and complexity of experience, the actual plot of *The 158-Pound Marriage* is relatively simple. But while the same might be said of the plots of *The Good Soldier* and *The Blood Oranges*, each of the earlier novels is more profoundly complex in its revelations—intentional or implicit—of the respective narrators. Irving's narrator is, on the other hand, not only unnamed, but remains, in many ways, far less affecting and effective than either Ford's Dowell or Hawkes's Cyril. Indeed, with this his third novel, Irving seems again to be searching for a central consciousness, a focusing vision which can assimilate, interpret, and develop saving insight into the comprehensive experience that his "I" narrates. And while in *Water-Method Man* Irving began to integrate often conflicting and ambivalent forces in Trumper far more effectively than he had been able to with Graff and Siggy in *Bears*, he appears to have reverted to a fragmented consciousness in *The 158-Pound Marriage*. For the narrator is not a fully realized character, even though we are unequivocally centered in his consciousness throughout the novel. In fact, far more interesting is Severin Winter, the narrator's antagonist and the magnetic, though rarely admirable, rival for the affections of the two women in the novel.

It is not, of course, unusual for a first-person narrator to be a relatively conservative observer of a far more explosive and apparently passionate protagonist, as Ishmael and Nick Carraway abundantly demonstrate. It is also true that the experiences of the narrators in both *The Good Soldier* and *The Blood Oranges* are partially shaped and revealed in the counterpoint of their relationships to their antagonists, characters who frequently function as doppelgängers or alter egos to the sharply contrasting personalities of the narrators. In significant ways, however, *The Great Gatsby* is Nick Carraway's story, just as *The Good Soldier* is Dowell's and *The Blood Oranges*, Cyril's.

What Irving fails to do in *The 158-Pound Marriage* is to create a multidimensional narrative persona who can convey or embody an artistically integrated human experience, an experience that should be embedded in the novel's structure and revealed through its narration. Instead, the novel seems schizophrenic—the dominant emotional energy and experience belonging to Severin, the point of view and implied focus resting in the anonymous and unrealized narrator. Irving does not achieve what he apparently intended: "I wanted to tell a tale by a villain . . . the least reliable, the one you can trust the least";[3] the narrator is more vulnerable than villainous and everyone in the novel is ultimately unreliable.

While this problem of focus is not in and of itself catastrophic, nor does it render *The 158-Pound Marriage* totally ineffectual, it is apparently an artistic problem that to this point plagued Irving's work. As we will argue later, the most successful resolution to date has manifested itself in the intricate narrative tapestry of *The World According to Garp*. Wanting the advantages of objectivity, detachment, and a kind of omniscience in the narrative voice without sacrificing the power of a central, fallible, and humanly limited character such as Garp, Irving chooses a far more effective mode of narration in his fourth novel. In *The 158-Pound Marriage*, his Garp-like character—minus the genuinely artistic sensibility—is basically fractured into *two* personalities: the quasiartist, seemingly objective (and mostly colorless) narrator, and the apparently wholly self-centered but perceptive and articulate Severin Winter. While Irving has it both ways in *Garp* (creating an omniscient third person narrator who also reveals Garp *directly*, through his art and letters), his earlier work, perhaps particularly *Marriage*, displays the artistic struggle he undergoes before he finds the vehicle to achieve synthesis.

"The Flaw in [Their] Footwork"

Assuming that full artistic focus and synthesis fail to occur in the novel, *The 158-Pound Marriage* nevertheless represents an interesting aspect of Irving's creative development. It is, for example, the first book that creates as a given the domestic world as a hermetic but wholly appropriate subject for art. While the resolution to Trumper's rootlessness and failure to make commitments may very well be his ultimate acceptance of a family and its joys and responsibilities, both *The Water-Method Man* and *Setting Free the Bears* deal primarily with picaresque figures who exist and experience life quite self-consciously apart from domestic entanglements. *Marriage*, on the other hand, is the first in a series of three novels whose most dramatic and psychologically profound experiences occur not only within the bosom of family but as a direct result of the immensely complex emotional forces Irving attributes to domestic relationships.

At the heart of this family hothouse are women and children. And while one could argue that Biggie, and particularly Tulpen, are treated with real sympathy by Irving, *Marriage* is the first novel in which Irving begins to introduce women as fully participating characters in the drama. Likewise, Severin Winter's relationship to and awareness of children as the key to emotional vulnerability and loss of rational control over one's life not only extends Trumper's concerns, but clearly adumbrates Garp's obsessions and the critical dynamic in the Berry family's experiences:

"It's about my children," he said. I had heard him talk about them a hundred times, almost always in wrestling terms; he called them his weakness, his imbalance, his blind side, his loophole, the flaw in his footwork, the mistakes he would always repeat and repeat, his one faulty move. Yet he could not imagine not having children. He said they were his substitute for an adventurous, explorative life. With children his life would always be dangerous; he was grateful for that, the perverse bastard! He said his love for Edith was almost rational (a matter of definition, I suppose), but that there was nothing reasonable about the way he loved his children. He said that people who didn't have children were naïve about the control they had over their lives. They always thought they were in control, or that they could be. (142)

The vulnerability that Severin describes as a natural consequence of his attachment to his children is not only a constant condition in Irving's work, it is an increasingly evident characteristic of his most sympathetic (and ultimately salvageable) characters, both men and women. Already in *Water-Method Man*, as we have seen, this condition is pronounced in Trumper, and serves as one indication of his potential for development. Therefore, the narrator of *Marriage*'s initial skepticism about and detachment from Severin's description of the fundamental irrationality and power of parent-child attachments is telling indeed, for his tenuous involvement with his own children is partially a result of other selfish preoccupations and of his failure to recognize their real importance to his life: "I admit that my own sense of family suffered from our foursome. I remember the children least of all, and this bothers me" (127). Late in the novel—and only after the ménage à quatre has been terminated—the narrator is jolted into awareness; when the Winters' children are seriously injured by shattering glass in the bathtub, he reacts: "With a shock . . . I realized that my Jack and my Bart had taken baths in that hazardous tub; I was thinking only that it could have happened to them, and that it could have been much worse" (233).

Utchka, on the other hand, whose own survival resulted from not only her widowed mother's sacrifice but also from the loving care of a Russian soldier, is far more self-consciously aware of her attachment to their children and of her husband's real, although until this point, unacknowledged priorities. As they drive home in silence after cleaning the Winters' house of the accident's debris, Utchka demonstrates her insight and causes the narrator to recognize his real affections: " 'Your children are more important to you than anything,' she said. I didn't answer, but it wasn't because I disagreed" (234).

Moreover, after Utchka takes their two sons to Vienna, the narrator's remorse clearly extends to his children, about whom he has frequent, ghoulish nightmares: "Then the dreams started and I couldn't sleep. They were about my children, and Severin Winter would have understood them" (248). Now clearly identifying with Severin's vulnerability, the narrator seems to be developing a potential for saving commitments and a possible domestic reconciliation. Perhaps symbolically signaling that end, as well as the centrality of children in the human drama, Irving has the narrator face the embarrassing irony that his "fifth historical novel," just published, is being distributed "as children's literature" (242).

With *Marriage*, then, the relationship of various characters to children in Irving's work begins to assume metaphoric as well as dramatic

status—a status that will shape the primary emotional experiences of
the next three novels and will actually culminate in *The Cider House
Rules*. Beginning the novel with Utchka's history, the narrator immediately recreates the horrific experiences of helpless Europeans facing
the onslaughts of Nazis and Russians alike by casting those experiences in a birth metaphor. He describes the deep attachment of
Utchka's mother to her lovely and helpless daughter which results in
a remarkable act of parental sacrifice and cunning designed to save the
child at all cost. Repeatedly raped and brutalized by both members of
the occupying armies and her own opportunistic neighbors, Utchka's
mother nevertheless: "cut open the belly of the cow, pulled out the
intestines and carved out the anus, and then made Utch lie down in
the cavity between the great cow's scooped-out ribs" (11). That the
girl is then literally "born" into the arms of a Russian officer, given
the name "calf" (Utchka), and raised by the surrogate "father" to
whom she was delivered "from the womb of the cow," establishes not
only the preternatural power of the "family" and the life cycle, but
also signals the narrator's symbolic (and perhaps unconscious) awareness of those same values and their relationship to his wife. That he
is slow to recognize their meaning for Severin and even slower for
himself, may indicate why, until he starts to write about his experiences: "I knew once again that I knew nothing" (254).

From Cows to Women

While the bovine imagery works effectively to introduce one of the
central thematic and symbolic patterns in *Marriage*, it has a less fortu-
nate effect in the way it serves to delimit Utchka as a potentially multidimensional character. As Miller rightly contends: "Unfortunately,
despite the fact that her past is well detailed, Utch does not emerge
as a convincing character during the course of the novel. . . . her
thoughts and responses in the midst of the affair remain too sketchy
to convey her development in character. It is a serious flaw in a book
whose central focus—and considerable achievement, in the cases of
the other three principals—is dynamic characterization."[4] An apolo-
gist for Irving could argue that the failure is the narrator's and not
the author's; for it is clear that the narrator's inability to see his wife
as a complex and suffering human being is one of his personal shortcomings and a root cause for the eventual dissolution of their relationship. As she unequivocally tells him: " 'You know *you*,' said Utch.

'That's all you know' " (240). But Irving cannot have it both ways: we must be given enough indirect information (through dialogue uninterpreted by the narrator, structural arrangements or symbolic detail) to make independent judgments about characters at the same time we see them primarily through the eyes of the "I." And what Irving does so successfully with Severin Winter (and to a lesser extent with Edith), he fails to do with Utchka: she remains at times unconvincing, and at others an undeveloped bovine figure much like Biggie in *The Water-Method Man.*

Edith, on the other hand, while a not wholly satisfactory or particularly attractive character, is imbued with a lively intelligence and a relatively complex psychological chemistry. As an aspiring writer who actually finishes a novel in the midst of the emotional maelstrom that temporarily dominates her life, Edith manifests a tough-mindedness Irving will later develop more fully in the persons of Jennie, Helen Holm, Franny, and Susie.

Given her Brahmin background ("the New York Fullers [never] needed a job" [31]), Edith's initial attraction to the charming but "crude and chivalrous" Severin seems a bit unlikely. Clearly blessed with some saving self-consciousness, however, Edith falls in love "because he was the first man who treated me lightly. . . . He simply found the comic ingredient in most things—even in me, and I took myself very seriously, of course" (46).

She also sees him as a "friendly animal" (46) and a "baby bear" (42), characterizations whose innocence and vulnerability will later in their marriage be belied by Severin's sexual betrayals and egotism. That Edith grows as a result of the quaternion and finally recognizes Severin for what he is and deals with him on her own terms, suggests an admirable strength and maturity the narrator never achieves, however much he insists on the similarities that bind them.

In contrast to Severin and Utch, Edith shares with the narrator a seeming indifference to her children, an indifference Severin never lets her forget: "he threw up the children so often to Edith, as if they were sacred objects she didn't adequately worship" (135). Indeed, Edith's apparent unawareness of her daughters reaches parodic proportions as she continuously fails to recognize which one of the two is addressing her. And while Irving increasingly attempts to draw female characters liberated from traditional and stereotypical associations, the failure to be sensitive to children is almost always symbolic

of a major moral failing and significant human flaw, whether the
character is male or female.

Whatever her shortcomings in this regard, Edith's attachment to
Severin is genuine and touching. Having apparently suffered considerably as a result of Severin's earlier infidelity, Edith is deeply disturbed
when she discovers that Severin has taken Utch to the scene of his
previous betrayal: " 'They went to the wrestling room.' Edith shiv-
ered and hugged herself; she looked as if she was going to be sick"
(184).

Edith's reaction to Severin's previous affair with Audrey Cannon is
not simply the jealous outrage of the sexually betrayed wife; she is
disturbed by the far more threatening possibility of Severin's emotional commitment to the maimed dancer: " 'But we just *talked*' Severin insisted. . . . 'Which is the worst kind of infidelity,' Edith said"
(195). Moreover, though they, too, "talked," her affection for Severin
is never seriously compromised by her affair with the narrator, despite
his illusions to the contrary. Imagining that Edith is suffering as he
is from the abrupt end of the relationship, the narrator tries to com-
fort her:

> "Utch and I hope we can see you again soon. I know it's going to be hard
> at first."
> "Not for me," she said brightly.
> "Oh."
> "Forget it," said Edith. "That's what I'm doing."
> But she didn't mean it. She was clearly insulating herself from her real
> feelings for me; she had to, no doubt, because of Severin's nonstop, needling
> ways. (217)

Just as he mistakenly attributes Edith's pain to her regret over losing him, the narrator also fails to understand the significance of
Edith's revenge on Severin. While she loves and is willing to forgive
her husband, Edith must assert her personal independence and ability
to wound him before she can re-enter the relationship. Her attempt
to seduce the young wrestler, George Bender, is not therefore an act
of simple cruelty so much as it is an assertion of her individuality: "I
wanted to teach [Severin] that he couldn't cram his life down my
throat and not leave me free to live mine" (226). Thus, while Edith
is perhaps not a fully realized character, she represents a new phase in
Irving's development: the self-directed, self-assured woman.

"His Ambition Was to Be a *Wife!*"

Like Utchka, Severin is first introduced by the narrator in "embry-
onic" form. Using Katrina Marek, the same actress character he created in *Setting Free the Bears*, Irving has her reappear in this novel in
an even more complicated role: as Severin's mother, "the Viennese actress Katrina Marek [who] the papers claim . . . was an 'astounding'
Antigone, which seems a suitable role for her to have played at the
time; she would have required loose garments for her costume, for she
was eight months pregnant with Severin" (20). Just as Utchka's
mother protects her daughter from the ravages of the Russian occupation by implanting her in the womb of a cow from which she is mi-
raculously reborn, Katrina performs a parallel action when she gets
"herself and her fetus out of the country" on the eve of the *Anschluss*.

Two startling coincidences, therefore, bind Utchka and Severin
from the beginning: they are symbolically and even literally associated
with, and escape probable extinction through, the efficacious protec-
tions of the womb; and, they are contemporaries (both actually born
in 1938) in the historical trauma of Austria's darkest days. And while
the narrator reluctantly agrees "they just had their war stories in common" (23), he nevertheless completely misses the profound significance of the connections: "Severin Winter . . . even had some history
in common with Utch, for all that it mattered. History occasionally
lies" (17).

The birth/rebirth metaphors that serve to link Severin and Utch
initially are conflated as the novel unfolds, unbeknown to the narrator
who unconsciously supplies the signals to the reader. From fetuses almost mythically protected, Utch and Severin emerge in analogous
form as fiercely protective "maternal" figures: "I think that, as a rule,
mothers are more serious than fathers. . . . But my theory breaks
down with Severin Winter. *He* was the mother in their family" (35).
And while Irving feels free to interchange the maternal/paternal metaphors (Severin oversees his wrestlers "like a father observing his children in some incubator phase" [188]), he gradually manipulates his
material to emphasize the androgynous nature of Severin's character
and of his consequently paradoxical appeal to others: " 'how I live
matters more than what I do. I have ambitions for the *quality* of how
I live; I have no ambitions for making money. I would prefer to have
my income provided, and in turn I would provide quality talk, quality food and quality sex!' . . . his ambition was to be a *wife!*" (118).

Being so unabashedly frank about what are traditionally "female" aspirations at the same time he thrives on typically masculine activities and posturings, Severin Winter becomes Irving's first multidimensional androgynous character and an obvious forerunner of Garp. Having already hinted at an androgynous figure in Couth, a key but secondary character in *The Water-Method Man*, Irving begins to demonstrate in *Marriage*—through androgyny as metaphor—an effective mode of dramatizing his vision and of embodying the paradox of the search for personal identity. For becoming fully human in Irving's universe increasingly depends on one's ability to transcend, however momentarily, an always indifferent, often violent world. And the ability to transcend that world depends, to a great extent, on the degree to which a genuine and thorough fusion of masculine and feminine impulses is achieved.

"A Benign Bomb"

Whatever his shortcomings (arrogance, self-indulgence, occasional cruelty), Severin Winter's ease in adapting to both the maternal and paternal, the masculine and feminine aspects of himself and of human experience, is a sign of his durability, his complexity, and finally his strength. Even in a humorous scene—which at first seems simply a typical example of Irving's comic hyperbole—Irving creates a virtual oxymoron to reinforce the androgynous image: "Severin Winter lay among [the four children] in Edith's gown, looking like a transvestite weight lifter dropped through the roof of an elementary school like a benign bomb" (132).

And, although the narrator occasionally appears cognizant of the existence of Severin's ambivalent nature and of its potential as a "benign bomb" (". . . Severin Winter's sense of family was more ferocious than most. We should all have been warned" [127]), he remains unalterably insensitive to the implications of Severin's androgynous vision as it illuminates the complex relationship with which they are all attempting to deal. Indeed, at precisely the moment the Winters choose to end the affair, the narrator characterizes Severin as the unfeeling, ruthless person his name would seem to symbolize: "His machine-steady gaze was as lifeless as the building he was entering: gray, concrete, steel and glass—its insides of chlorinated water, disinfected mats, ice frozen by cooling pipes, ointments and powders which dealt harshly with fungi of the feet and crotch, and countless bouncing balls pumped full of air. That was Severin Winter's world, and I knew I did not belong in it" (211). The "transvestite weight-lifter" insight is simply not compatible with the condemnation this latter judgment embodies. That Severin is capable of cruel, selfish, thoughtless, and egotistical acts is undeniable. That he is utterly mechanistic and monochromatic is, however, a simplistic rationaliza-tion of a desperately jealous and perhaps equally selfish man.

Moreover, the narrator seriously underestimates Severin's complex personality and its inevitable ability to affect other people's lives and emotions. Even when Utchka "claimed he was the only man she'd ever known who actually treated women as if they were equal to men" (84), the narrator persists in viewing Severin as a mindless, soulless jock whose sensibility is as limited as the space that is the wrestling room: "I don't think he saw anything clearly. Outside the wrestling room, out in the real world, he had no vision. He saw and thought and acted clearly under the moonlit dome, within the clear circles in-scribed on the wrestling mats, but he left his mind behind whenever he hung up his clothes in his locker" (197).

But Severin *does* see some things quite clearly outside the wrestling room—far more clearly than the narrator does. From the very begin-ning of the ménage à quatre, Severin articulates his fears: "I guess I feel that I have to do the worrying for all of us . . . because no one else seems worried about anything" (71). And while he hypocritically indulges himself in the sensual and ego-gratifying pleasures of the af-fair, and while he is not sympathetic enough to the pain of others, Severin ultimately has the most perceptive and realistic view of the experience and of the dynamics of healing the mutually inflicted wounds: " 'Look,' he said, '[Utch] just needs to get her pride back. I know, because I have to get my pride back, too. It's really very simple. She knows I didn't really want the whole thing, and she knows you were thinking more about yourself than about her. We were all thinking more about ourselves than about Utch' " (245).

"Eyes for Detail"

The narrator, on the other hand, has few such insights. Indeed, for one who repeatedly claims he has "eyes for detail" (16), the narrator's inability to anticipate the consequences of the quaternion and to accu-rately assess his real importance to his three counterparts provides striking evidence of "narrator as fool" or "I" as blind eye.

Recognizing the need to provide the reader with clues to the relative unreliability of his "I" narrator, Irving first creates a series of superficial signals which are designed to affect our judgment from the outset. The narrator is both nameless and, in Irving's world of "baby bear" physiques, physiologically suspect: "I am tall and thin; even my beard is narrow" (87). He is also something of a pontificator who arrogantly and simultaneously posits aesthetic theory and glibly generalizes about human complexity: "an unhappy man cannot tolerate a happy woman" (17).

Furthermore, and particularly meaningful when reviewing Irving's work retrospectively, the narrator is an historical novelist, a status in Irving somewhat akin to being a blind photographer. To argue that "people regard art too highly, and history not enough" (17) is a position unequivocally antithetical to Irving's own commitment to the imagined life of the genuine artist.

Unfortunately, however, these signals, or attempts at creating objective correlatives, are basically extrinsic to the novel itself and are glaringly obvious in their implications only to those who are already familiar with Irving's vision and prejudices as they are more fully realized in later novels. It is not, after all, immediately apparent that an underweight historical novelist without a name is necessarily an ironic or unreliable figure. It is perhaps a weakness of the novel that Irving relies too heavily on these cues to establish the context within which we are to filter and interpret the narrator's observations and judgments.

Other material that seems intended to guide the reader's perceptions is frequently confusing or, at best, ambiguous. Take, for example, the typical statements about art and the historical novel that the narrator posits: "We historical novelists know that the past can be vivid; it can even seem real" (170); or, "but we historical novelists are aware of how carelessly good intentions are regarded" (65). While clichés of a sort, these are not attitudes that are either reinforced or rejected by the artistic gestalt in which they are embedded. It is therefore difficult to draw conclusions from them about the narrator's reliability or integrity as an observer. In *The World According to Garp*, on the other hand, Garp's aesthetic statements are tested in relation to his art and are measured in a context that allows us to evaluate their (and Garp's) reliability.

In *Marriage*, the contradictory nature of some of these generalizations leads us to assume that the narrator's intellectual insight and ability to understand the experiences he and others undergo is itself confused or misleading.[5] Having dismissed as insignificant the bonding that history creates between Severin and Utch, for example, the narrator inexplicably asserts his contrary belief that art is regarded too highly, "history not enough." Condemning Severin for claiming "that he could love a person's past" because "we historical novelists are rarely as sentimental" (194), the narrator, in his despair over losing everyone he holds dear, dons his wife's slip and dresses the kitchen chairs in the children's clothes, the touching acts of a not unsentimental wallower in his own history, his own past.

Putting on Wooden Clogs

Perhaps the real key to Irving's narrator is provided not, however, by this collection of self-contradictory aesthetic statements or reflections on history and art, but by what becomes a controlling metaphor in the book: Bruegel's famous painting *The Fight between Carnival and Lent*. The painting and the narrator's interpretation of it and close identification with one of its principal figures helps illuminate various experiences in the novel as well as the narrator himself. The importance of the painting in the novel also demonstrates how frequently Irving uses artistic or creative works—Siggy's journal, the old Norse ballad *Akthelt and Gunnel*, the film *Fucking Up*, numerous short stories—as vehicles for dramatizing a character's psychology without the self-reflexive results he objects to so strenuously in much contemporary fiction: for example, the narrator's argument that "when the subject of fiction became how to write fiction, we lost interest; we were interested in prose, surely, but not when the subject of the prose became prose itself" (79).

The Fight between Carnival and Lent is first referred to by the narrator in the midst of a dialogue with Utch that is, for him, excruciatingly painful. Utch describes, in enthusiastic detail, the orgiastic experience she has just had with Severin in the wrestling room, home of Severin's conquests and betrayals—the circumscribed place where he exercises an almost exquisite psychological and physical control over lovers and wrestlers. Utch's obvious enjoyment of the experience and her "placidity among the toast crusts and yolk stains" drives the narrator into an escapist contemplation of the Bruegel masterpiece: "I lost myself in an image from years before. I imposed myself on

Bruegel's painting. I walked into his cosmos; I shrank, put on wooden clogs, browsed through the old Netherlandish town" (157).

Identifying with neither of the focal allegorical figures Lent or Carnival, the narrator nevertheless recognizes himself as "the well-dressed one":

> A well-to-do burgher? Possibly a patrician? I have never identified my station exactly. I am in a black tunic, fur-lined, expensive; my hair is cut like a scholar's; a rich purse hangs at my chest, a richly bound prayer book protrudes from my pocket; my cap is soft leather. I pass a blind man, but he is more than blind; appallingly, he is without eyes! . . . Without looking at him, I give him a coin. . . . Actually, I'm the only one in the painting who clearly isn't a peasant, the only one who has a servant. . . . I think I must be a lawyer, or maybe the mayor. (158–59)

Choosing this particular figure with whom to identify is telling indeed, for the painting abounds with interesting possibilities among the dozens of types it depicts. The choice, however, tells us a great deal about the narrator's sense of himself, or perhaps, about his self-delusions, for the obviously affluent burgher (*not* shod in clogs) is the most dignified and socially prominent secular figure in the painting. In addition, if one were to adopt the traditional view of Bruegel's work—that it represents the forces of Christian virtue (Lent) in combat with the raucous vices and indulgences of the devil (Carnival)—then clearly this generous burgher is staunchly aligned with the figures and gestures of *caritas*.

More complex views of Bruegel's painting and its symbolic significance (views with which Irving would no doubt sympathize) have, however, recently emerged. The painting does not, after all, display an unequivocal vision of either Carnival or Lent: neither of the major figures is particularly attractive nor is either of their retinues presented without complex and ambiguous associations. Bruegel "certainly shows little respect for either lovers or opponents of Carnival. . . . Two corpses . . . suggest that if it were not for the fear of death no one would bother to be charitable or even religious."[6]

A close study of the painting—a study Irving obviously made given the detail with which the narrator discusses it—reveals a multitude of ironic juxtapositions between and among characters and self-contained proverbial scenes which suggest Bruegel's mode as consciously ambiguous. The narrator's burgher, for instance, is piously passing alms to a blind man whom he fails even to acknowledge in some individualized way. The distorted figures in Carnival's retinue are no more or less grotesque than Lent or her retainers; and the churchgoers, usually considered appropriately pious, are actually presented suspiciously as death-masks, one even as a "prisoner" incarcerated behind his own prayer stool.

Beggars, cripples, and a myriad of maimed figures crowd the scene, apparently to be pitied and assisted. But the painting does not reflect a simple view of these helpless souls. There is even some suggestion that they overwhelm the community with their demands and needs and that some—the syphilitics, for example—are as much victimizers as victims, as much sinners as sinned against.

The narrator of *Marriage*, however, has little sensitivity to the paradoxes or ironies in Bruegel's painting and fails to consider other more apt figures with whom to identify than the burgher. Indeed, as he reminisces about his original plans for converting the painting into his "second historical novel," he reinforces the identification with the burgher: "At one point in the novel, my characters would all come together and be doing just what they're doing in the painting. I had already selected the well-to-do man with the prayer book in his pocket to be me, to be the narrator of the book" (159).

As Miller points out, the prominent and central figures in the painting are ignored by the narrator,[7] and yet they may represent the most appropriate analogues for the novel's characters: an unidentifiable couple (whose sexual identity is not even altogether clear) being led away from the moral psychodrama by a fool. The couple's movement away from the impending battle between Carnival and Lent might suggest the reluctance with which the couples in the novel face up to the human and moral questions their affair raises. Furthermore, if Irving is using the painting as a kind of objective correlative, he may be far more interested in presenting the narrator's omission of these figures than he is in making any statements about the battle between the equally unattractive forces of Carnival and Lent.

It is also noteworthy that the narrator planned, in 1963, to title his "historical novel" *Carnival's Quarrel with Lent* and that he imagines writing it from the point of view of "my unidentified character, the lost burgher" (249). If this is so, Irving would seem to suggest, the perspective is self-deluding and the narrator, as lost burgher, misses the central significance of the story he tells.

The Lost Burgher

Although there is little hard evidence that the narrator's desires to reunite himself with Utch and to "try the Bruegel book again" are anything more than fantasies, the novel we read is a retrospective narrative and has perhaps served not only as an emotional catharsis but as a vehicle to self-discovery, much as Trumper's account clearly does. Unfortunately, however, the only hint we get that suggests such self-discovery is even possible for the obtuse narrator is his final self-assessment: "I knew once again that I knew nothing." Although this self-awareness may be the ideal prerequisite for personal epiphany to occur as a function of performing the artistic act—creation as discovery—little else in the novel reinforces such a pattern.

It would be easy and charitable to suggest that Irving exerted the kind of conscious artistic control over his material that could turn an ostensibly confused canvas into an ironically self-reflective exposé of a weak and deluded man turned perceptive self-mocker through the medium of the "Bruegel book" he writes. And while one may perhaps make that claim for Trumper and for Ford's Dowell (and make a different, but equally strong claim for Hawkes's Cyril), *The 158-Pound Marriage* does not resolve into artistic closure, even into purposefully ambiguous closure as its literary predecessors do.

And although his third novel is, superficially at least, very different from his first, Irving's "sense of an ending" is no more sure in *The 158-Pound Marriage* than it was in *Setting Free the Bears*. Having found a successful way to deal with similar narrative and structural problems in *The Water-Method Man*, Irving seems to lose that emerging control in *The 158-Pound Marriage*.[8]

What does emerge from this novel, however, are several important emphases and themes which become increasingly significant in the next two works: the complexity and richness of the domestic milieu; the potentially transcendent quality of the androgynous figure; art and the artistic act as metaphor; and the existentially meaningful possibilities of creation as discovery. In *The World According to Garp*, Irving will shape these developing materials into a classic novel of our time.

Chapter Five
The World According to
Garp: Life as a Doomed
Effort at Reclassification

In the four years following the publication of what must be considered his least successful novel, *The 158-Pound Marriage*, a still youthful Irving conceived and brilliantly executed his masterpiece, *The World According to Garp*. Previous struggles with point of view, clarity, tone, and breadth of canvas resolved themselves—by the mysterious processes that shape an artist's sensitivity and capacity to create a superbly realized work—in a novel whose voice, structure, and vision define it as a unique expression of "true" (as opposed to "real")[1] human experience.

As powerful and artistically satisfying as it is, however, *The World According to Garp* was nevertheless a struggle to write: "I had a shaky time in the early going with it—it was raggedly put together, and I feel about it a little like a tailor who sees somebody walking away in a suit that everybody else says looks like a good suit, but they can't see the seams, but he remembers how many times he had to cut the pant-leg, you know what I mean? . . . But *I* see the seams—I know that the *making* of that book was not a smooth and satisfying event. . . ."[2]

It is possible, of course, that the difficult and frustrating process Irving describes through the tailor metaphor offers precisely the key to the novel's brilliance; painstaking editing and obsessive concern with construction and structure are everywhere felt in the complex architecture and intricate tailoring of *The World According to Garp*. As Garp says of his mother, Jenny Fields's "messy" book: "My mother never knew about the silence of revision" (124); in this case, Irving apparently did.

Irving's fourth novel is a long, multilayered, elaborately designed, and intricately narrated story of a man, an artist, a family, a generation—an entire cosmos in the Dickensian sense. It is a novel whose center is T. S. Garp but whose implications and scope stretch in all directions far beyond the brief life of the protagonist. For, in this novel, Irving breaks away from the comfortable mode of contemporary, often solipsistic or self-reflexive fiction and resurrects—simultaneously forging anew—the bold, teeming-with-life "traditional" novel which we most often associate with the British in the last two centuries.

Whether or not Irving intentionally chose—as he later did in *The Cider House Rules*—to emulate the technique of his literary ancestors is not altogether clear; he is, after all, a self-described student of earlier fiction: "I'm very well read in the eighteenth and nineteenth centuries. . . ."[3] But it is obvious from the opening line of the novel that, while the subject is Garp, a fictionalized history will be presented: "Garp's mother, Jenny Fields, was arrested in Boston in 1942 for wounding a man in a movie theater" (1). Thus, Garp's "prehistory" begins. Moreover, the extended framework of the narrative is no surprise either: listed immediately after the dedication, the table of contents leaves no doubt as to the traditional mode and little hope of "happy endings": chapter 19 of the novel is titled "Life After Garp."

Irving thereby signals his readers that the story of Garp will be embedded in an "historical" framework which both pre- and postdates him: the novel will, by definition, focus considerable attention on other characters. Much like traditional biography, it will emphasize family and other immediate relationships—relationships which serve to define and illuminate T. S. Garp and his world.

"The Seed of a Ball Turret Gunner"

The World According to Garp begins with one of the most exuberant, bizarre, and ironically comic chapters in recent fiction. T. S. Garp's mother, Jenny Fields, is introduced and the story of her fierce nonconformity and independence—from most men and from the largely hypocritical values of a New England upperclass family—is instantly evoked by her joint desires to work in the declassé profession of nursing and to have a baby without the acceptable accoutrements: "I wanted a job and I wanted to live alone. . . . Then I wanted a baby, but I didn't want to have to share my baby or my life to have one" (15).

Against all logic, training, and social opinion, Jenny chooses a terminally injured Technical Sergeant (the time is 1942) to father her child by combining an act of mercy with a benign rape: stimulating the fetallike soldier, Jenny virtually impregnates herself with his "absurdly fertile" (27) sperm from which T. S. Garp will inevitably (we know) emerge: "born from a good nurse with a will of her own, and the seed of a ball turret gunner—his last shot" (31).

Raising her precocious child alone, Jenny becomes head nurse of the Steering School, cunningly combining her profession and commitment to offer Garp a first-class education. Growing up at Steering, Garp will encounter the two families whose members will play critical and continuing roles in his life (and premature death): The Percys (and their vicious, anthropomorphic dog, Bonkers) and the Holms. While the Percys and their extensive (and clearly genetically weakened) clan represent the same fatuous New England class Jenny's own family embodies, the Holms—Helen and her wrestling coach father, Ernie—come to symbolize the unpretentious, bright and caring nontraditional family which mirrors and supports Jenny and Garp's existence and values. That Garp will traffic with both a Percy daughter and Helen Holms is, too, inevitable. That that trafficking will ultimately shape his entire adult experience is one of the ways the world according to Irving is given existential and artistic form.

It is at Steering that Garp will decide to marry Helen and will identify his lifetime vocation and avocation: writing and wrestling. And, despite Helen's no-nonsense evaluation of the first short story he has the temerity to share with her ("at this point, you are more of a wrestler than a writer" [93]), he is true to his self-described destiny regardless of the sacrifices—for himself and others—his choices will exact.

His life at Steering is, however, less than idyllic; for as in much of Irving's fiction, the seeds of discontent, the forces of inevitability, are often and irrevocably planted and put into motion in the seemingly innocuous events and relationships of adolescence. Just so with Garp: while he gets his revenge on Bonkers for inflicting a childhood injury, and successfully enjoys his first real sexual experience with Cushie Percy, these activities will not be simply the normal processes of maturation for which few of us pay a dear price, but will establish a metaphorically predetermined chain of associations that ultimately demand an ironic form of poetic justice and come to define the fragile condition of existence in Irving's world.

"In the Life of a Man, His Time Is But a Moment"

Garp is a tender eighteen-year-old when he and Jenny embark on their trip to Vienna in 1961, confident that a budding writer can benefit from what Mr. Tinch, Garp's English instructor, calls the "c-c-contemplative and artistic" world of Europe. Garp is not only dismayed that his mother "meant to stay *with* him" but also that she intends "writing something" herself (107).

Despite Jenny's almost maddening productivity at the typewriter and his own inability to write, Garp is nevertheless artistically stimulated in the new environment; he perceptively recognizes the qualities of Vienna that act to trigger his maturation: "Vienna was in its death phase; it lay still and let me look at it, and think about it, and look again. In a *living* city, I could never have noticed so much. Living cities don't hold still" (123). Combining his own insights with the intellectual lessons he learns about the brevity and transience of human experience from Marcus Aurelius—in the life of man, his time is but a moment—Garp begins an unusual and artful story titled "The Pension Grillparzer," one of three stories that Irving will share directly with his readers. Initially unable to complete the piece because he "knew he did not know enough; not yet" (155), Garp chooses instead to resubmerge himself in the experiential riches Vienna has to offer, most notably in the life of rarified pleasure to which Charlotte, a first-district prostitute of whom Jenny has reluctantly approved, has exposed him. Then watching Charlotte die of a cancer that has attacked the very vehicle of her profession ("they cut my purse out" [162]), Garp is faced for the first time with the "*dream* of death" (139) made manifest in his reality: he is able to complete "The Pension Grillparzer" because "now he knew what the . . . dream meant" (167). The ironic juxtaposition of sex and death—a juxtaposition central to Irving's vision and native to Vienna—will continue to inspire Garp as artist much as it will haunt him as man.

"It Is Rich with Lunacy and Sorrow"

Returning to New England, Garp marries Helen (Ph.D. in English literature at twenty-three), begins a family (with the understanding that he will care for the children while Helen pursues her academic career), and starts writing in earnest. He is ironically assisted in this life because "Jenny took care of the money" (183), a convenience made possible by his mother's own quite remarkable success with the massive book (aptly titled *A Sexual Suspect*) she wrote in Vienna. For while Garp was attempting to experience life and to master a delicate craft, Jenny was indiscriminately churning out "the first truly feminist autobiography" (185), a characterization she neither intended nor supports, despite her enormous and unpremediated social and financial success.

Learning to live with Jenny's "artistic" and, increasingly, political fame (and soon to follow, public notoriety), Garp is thrust into a world where women dominate his life and consciousness and where acute awareness of the victimization of women—most potently symbolized by rape—is, for him, in constant and irresolvable tension with the lust he continues to feel (and periodically acts upon) for baby-sitters, other men's wives, and assorted other women. Despite his genuine love for Helen and his virtually obsessive commitment to his two sons, Garp occasionally (and guiltily) indulges his lust at the same time he writes two moderately well-reviewed novels and engages in a love-hate relationship with a variety of feminist types, many of whom quickly identify him as the enemy. Made a "hero" for swiftly apprehending the rapist of a young girl, Garp is nevertheless despised and ridiculed by lunatic fringe feminists who have cut out their own tongues in stupid acts of symbolic identification with a rape and mutilation victim named Ellen James.

Caught in a world where absurd violence abounds and traditional sexual roles and identities are no longer literally or psychologically viable (Garp's best friend is a transsexual named Roberta Muldoon, formerly tight end for the Philadelphia Eagles), Garp struggles to create a wholesome, vital family life and simultaneously to create art in which "laughter was related to sympathy" (232) and in which "he had . . . imagined far enough beyond his own fairly ordinary experience" (238). That Garp's "official biography" will later be titled *Lunacy and Sorrow: The Life and Art of T. S. Garp* (589) is, therefore, hardly surprising since the paradox of compassionate comedy is at the root of Garp's personal life and artistic vision.

Experiencing mounting frustration because he feels unable to realize this vision, however (" 'You're suffering a crisis of confidence about your *writing*,' Helen told him" [253]), Garp grows increasingly self-indulgent and overbearing with Helen and the children alike and inadvertently creates an environment in which the seeds of tragedy are easily sown.

"The Leer of the World"

While Irving does not literally separate *The World According to Garp* into two major parts, the novel's infrastructure and tone shift direction and divide the narrative in subtle and compelling ways.[4] For in roughly the first half of the novel (chapters 1–11), there is considerably more lunacy than sorrow; whereas, in the second half (chapters 12–19), sorrow (always accompanied by a liberal dose of lunacy) predominates, often taking the metaphoric form of the ubiquitous "Under Toad," the malapropism younger son Walt invents for the "undertow" of which he is repeatedly warned to beware.

In the second half of the novel, a violent and devastating chain of events is precipitated when Helen succumbs to the lust which has, until this point, far more intensively beleaguered Garp. Partially rationalizing her attraction to an arrogant and effete graduate student named Michael Milton by blaming Garp for his restlessness and self-indulgence, Helen proceeds—rather cold-bloodedly—to engage in an affair that has far greater meaning for Milton than for her. When Garp discovers the relationship, the pain and egotism of his reaction trigger a bizarre and tragic automobile accident in which Walt is killed, Duncan, the elder son, loses an eye, and Helen, ironically attempting to extricate herself from the relationship with Milton by a final act of sexual mercy, accidentally mutilates him by biting off his penis. The devastation wrought leaves the remaining family members physically injured and in a state of profound psychic shock which is ministered to by the dauntless Jenny playing her most beloved roles as nurse and mother. The rehabilitation occurs at Dog's Head Harbor, the Fields family estate on the New Hampshire coast, lately converted to a sanctuary for victimized women with whom the Garps will now share their recuperation.

Garp's personal trauma is accompanied by an artistic trauma which, both literally and figuratively, leaves him voiceless—for the accident broke his jaw, mangled his tongue, and left him physically speechless, much as he had already become, he believes, bereft of an artistic voice. Having last written a moribund and unimaginative story titled "Vigilance" (the second of the three stories presented in toto in the novel), Garp now finds himself artistically paralyzed.

Forced to write notes to communicate to his family and the other guests at Dog's Head Harbor, Garp is savagely and ironically associated with the self-mutilated Ellen Jamesians, a group for whom he continues to feel undisguised contempt.

Gradually, however, Garp begins the painful process of concocting a new novel, one which will be full of the "leer of the world" (328), yet which will ultimately serve as therapy and will help provide the healing he so desperately requires to reconstruct his life as man and artist.

"In Garp's Work, Guilt Always Abounds"

The first chapter of Garp's third novel, *The World According to Bensenhaver*, is reproduced as chapter 15 of *The World According to Garp*. An absolutely horrific story of kidnapping, rape, and grotesque murder committed in self-defense, it is greeted by Garp's publisher, the intelligent and caring John Wolf, as a kind of literary obscenity deserving to be published in no loftier a journal than *Crotch Shots*. Wolf is startled, however, when his very secret and unofficial reader, an uneducated cleaning woman named Jillsy Sloper, reacts positively to the complete novel: "It feels so *true*. . . . A book's true when you can say, 'Yeah! That's just how damn people *behave* all the time.' *Then* you know it's true" (453). Wolf then will publish the novel and its success will provide the financial independence Garp wants: "Garp actually felt that he could buy a sort of isolation from the real and terrible world" (442).

Partly as a function of writing the new novel, Garp is able finally to forgive Helen, exorcise his own guilt, and reconcile himself to life in "the real and terrible world." Eventually, Helen—"who'd been made to suffer disproportionately for a trivial indiscretion" (380)— is also able to reconcile herself to the past and make an affirmative commitment: she and Garp have another child, a daughter whom they aptly name Jenny Garp.

After the new baby is born, and just before *The World According to Bensenhaver* is published, the Garps, including partially blind but artistic Duncan, embark on a trip to Vienna—a trip designed to consummate the cleansing ritual they have undergone. Much as he felt uneasy on his first trip to Vienna, however, Garp again "felt the Under Toad was strong" (457). Inevitably, his instincts prove accurate; Roberta calls with the news that Jenny, while campaigning for a woman gubernatorial candidate, has been fatally shot by an antifeminist deer hunter. Grief-stricken, the family returns to America "in the airplane that was bringing [Garp] home to be famous in his violent country" (486).

"Garp Was Guilty of Unnecessary Roughness"

Undaunted in his desire to attend Jenny's memorial service, "the first feminist funeral in New York," Garp allows Roberta to disguise him in drag and act as his bodyguard at the funeral. Having already alienated the Ellen Jamesians and many other radical feminists, Garp, when he is identified by Pooh Percy (youngest daughter of the Steering Percy clan and sister of Cushie, Garp's adolescent lover), causes pandemonium. He must literally run for his life. As he flees, he meets the real Ellen James, a sensitive young woman writer who disassociates herself totally from her crude imitators and expresses her affection for Garp's novels and life. Recently orphaned, Ellen accepts Garp's offer of a family and is ultimately adopted by them: "One-eyed and no tongued, thought Garp, my family will pull together" (514).

Returning to Steering ("the only place I know" [520]) with his newly extended family, Garp discovers Helen's father, Ernie, and Stewart Percy, scion of the dreadful Percy family, both recently dead. The old life and its parent figures—Jenny, Ernie, and "Fat Stew"—will be replaced by the next generation, living in and renovating the Percy mansion and devoting themselves to familiar preoccupations. Made financially independent through Jenny's legacy and the commercial success of *The World According to Bensenhaver*, Garp volunteers his services as Steering's wrestling coach and Helen eventually returns to teaching there.

While Garp the artist struggles to regain "the freedom of *imagining* life truly" (522) without much success, the family's otherwise placid existence is nevertheless fulfilling, particularly as Garp at first reluctantly—and then with some enthusiasm—dedicates himself to helping victimized women through the auspices of the "Fields Foundation," pleasing Roberta who had earlier made the painfully accurate assessment that: "There's such sympathy for people, in what you *write*. . . . But I don't see that much sympathy in you, in your real life" (383).

But at the same time he provides funds and emotional support for an array of unfortunate women, he and Ellen James wage a very public and savage epistolary war with the Ellen Jamesians which leaves Garp: "In his own wrestling terminology . . . guilty of unnecessary roughness. . . . He was a man who had publicly lost his temper; he had demonstrated that he could be cruel" (556). And while Garp "did not share [Helen's] sense of the Under Toad—not this time" (551), it is very near in the person of an Ellen Jamesian "aiming the Saab at Garp" (557), who barely misses him, killing herself instead.

Perhaps as a result of this narrow (and temporary) escape from the Under Toad, Garp begins writing again, both a novel called *My Father's Illusions* (a story not unlike Irving's *The Hotel New Hampshire*) and surprisingly charitable letters to magazines apologizing for "the vehemence and self-righteousness of his remarks" (562). However, "apologies are rarely acceptable to true believers" (562), and with every bit of the inevitability of a Dreiser or Norris scenario, Garp faces the Under Toad in his wrestling room womb with Helen present, as she always has been. A tongueless nurse figure with "a Jenny Fields Original . . . sewn over the breast" (573), Pooh Percy, delirious in her irrational hatred of men, fatally shoots the man who, in her warped fantasy, is the consummate symbol of the enemy.

"Life After Garp"

In an interesting manipulation of traditional literary forms, Irving kills Garp off not in the penultimate chapter of the novel, but in the final chapter, "Life After Garp," which begins with the lines: "He loved epilogues. . . . 'An epilogue,' Garp wrote, 'is more than a body count. An epilogue, in the disguise of wrapping up the past, is really a way of warning us about the future' " (567).

We have known all along Garp will die a premature and probably violent death—the only mystery is how and by whose hand. And in his own masterful epilogue, Irving demonstrates how close at hand, how "familiar" death ultimately is:

It surprised him to realize that the Under Toad was no stranger, was not even mysterious; the Under Toad was very familiar—as if he had always known it, as if he had grown up with it. It was yielding, like the warm wrestling mats; it smelled like the sweat of clean boys—and like Helen, the first and last woman Garp loved. The Under Toad, Garp knew now, could even look like a nurse: a person who is familiar with death and trained to make practical responses to pain. (575)

After portraying Garp's murder—"a death scene, John Wolf told Jillsy Sloper, that only Garp could have written" (576)—Irving begins the "real" epilogue (an epilogue within an epilogue) "warning us about the future" as "T. S. Garp might have imagined it" (577), and in a brilliant tour de force of barely thirty pages, details the lives (and often maimings or deaths) of virtually every major figure in the Garpian/Dickensian menagerie. That he ends the epilogue, and hence the novel, with Jenny Garp, an androgynous female figure whose symbolic presence (since she is never developed as a "character" in any novelistic sense) provides an emblematic celebration of Garp's life and legacy, is Irving's ultimate paradox. Jenny, a doctor who "had a writer's sense of immortality" (608), is to engage in cancer research and, like her father, in effect die in a paradoxical relationship to her calling: "she hoped she would get to the bottom of cancer. In a sense, she would. She would die of it" (608).

Fascinated by the parallel experiences of artist and doctor (an analogy Irving will develop extensively in *The Cider House Rules*), Jenny "liked to describe herself as her father had described a novelist. 'A doctor who sees only terminal cases' " (609). Also like her father— and like their mutual creator—Jenny will celebrate life despite its inevitable horrors: "Jenny Garp would outlive them all" (607).

"Helen Taught a Course in Narrative Point of View"

A full understanding of *The World According to Garp* requires a thorough familiarity with its complex narrative, bold themes, and Dickensian cast of often eccentric but vital characters. The foregoing (and relatively lengthy) summary, however, does not pretend to exhaust the novel's richness, demonstrate its exuberance and Rabelaisian ribaldry, or illuminate the nature and importance of its narrative mode. In order to appreciate fully the genuine artistry of the novel, it is essential to understand through what prisms Irving refracts the experiences of *The World According to Garp*. Indeed, Irving is perhaps intentionally cuing us to the significance of the novel's perspective when, without the sarcasm he generally reserves for the obsessions of professors of literature, he describes the course Helen is teaching when her fatal affair with Michael Milton begins: "Helen was interested in the development and sophistication of narrative technique, with special attention to point of view, in the modern novel" (312).

As we described it briefly in the introductory chapter to this study, the apparently traditional, virtually omniscient third person narrative of *Garp* is interestingly modified by Irving to include direct, unfiltered access to Garp's sensibility by presenting several short stories and letters directly to us without the interpreting mediation of the narrative voice—a voice that, in other parts of the novel, is ubiquitous and has an almost godlike command of his materials. Unabashedly moving in and out of whatever consciousness he chooses to reveal at a given moment (though focusing primarily on Garp), the narrator is nevertheless utterly "objective" when he presents Garp's stories and letters in full rather than through paraphrase or other filtering devices.

Unlike Thackeray, who never lets us forget the "artifice" he is creating or Fielding whose narrative persona has a distinctive, if sardonic, personality, Irving's narrator—while rarely offering value judgments—occasionally inserts an interpretive comment that cannot conceivably emanate from any of the characters themselves. When, for example, after he shares with us the amusing (and aesthetically significant) exchange of letters between Garp and the philistine Irene Poole, the narrator comments: "Thus was his sense of humor lost, and his sympathy taken from the world" (237), that judgment (and the immediately following paragraph evaluating "The Pension Grillparzer") represents a narrative intrusion in which he rarely indulges. Though one might argue that Irving simply makes a "mistake" here (and in the few other places the narrator slips out of individual consciousnesses and into a discrete voice of his own), it is more likely that Irving is intentionally calling our attention to a figure who does indeed have an identity as separate from the author himself as he clearly is from Garp throughout. And while the argument is often persuasively made that earlier practitioners of selective or wholly omniscient narratives worked at distancing themselves from their storytelling personas, Irving may well feel the demands of a world shrunken away from assumed godlike postures far more sharply than did the Hawthorne of "The Custom House," the Thackeray of *Vanity Fair*, or even the "invisible" Joyce of *Ulysses*. For however adroitly Irving evokes the traditions of the novel and the romance, he is preeminently a man and writer grounded in the contemporary world where the limitations of knowledge and insight must be embodied and acknowledged even in the most apparently omniscient of voices. In leavening the tradition he evokes, Irving establishes himself to that extent as an experimentalist in the form of the novel.

"The Adventurer's Instinct in Narration"

While the first two pages of *The World According to Garp* ostensibly establish the tone and technique of the objective biographer who deftly sketches the indomitable Jenny's early life and present dilemma in matter-of-fact, even journalistic form, these same two pages illuminate a method that will quite subtly affect our willingness to accept the narrator as a credible, even sympathetic, observer of Garp and his world. The narrator quickly demonstrates two sources of knowledge: the first, a "public" source, is Jenny's book; he adds what is perhaps the typical parenthetical qualifier of the traditional biographer: "(later she wrote, in her famous autobiography, that too many nurses put themselves on display for too many doctors; but then her nursing days were over)" (2).

More interesting, the narrator unobtrusively inserts another reference in the form of a quote which would seem to reinforce his credibility: " 'My mother,' Garp wrote, 'was a lone wolf' " (2). Our reaction may simply be to accept the narrator's authority as one who has carefully studied Garp's writings and who, by the end of the first chapter, will have quoted Garp a dozen times and Jenny's autobiography, *A Sexual Suspect*, only several times fewer.

This technique, of course, can be a purely fictional device Irving uses to establish the narrator's reliability and omniscience; a godlike, traditional third person "puppeteer" need not prove he has any mortal responsibility for establishing his credibility or the source of his knowledge—one can easily concede Irving this convention.

If, however, an important aspect of Irving's method and approach to form in the novel is not merely to reinvigorate traditional techniques but to reshape them in ways that more accurately embody and reflect an existential vision of experience that cannot be entirely denied, mediated, or transcended, then his narrator may be a very "real" voice artistically shaping materials to which only he has absolute (and thereby irrefutable) access. Such a figure potentially exists in *The World According to Garp* but is not introduced until the last chapter of the novel: "His name was Donald Whitcomb, and his nervous stutter reminded Garp, affectionately, of the departed Mr. Tinch. . . ." (569).

Meeting Garp for the first time on the day he will be murdered in the wrestling room, Whitcomb, "who adored Garp's work" (569) is the unlikely recipient of Garp's most private thoughts about the nature of fiction and of life—thoughts Garp had previously shared di-

rectly with no one but Helen: "Don Whitcomb would remember that
Garp told him what the act of starting a novel felt like. 'It's like trying to make the dead come alive,' he said. 'No, no, that's not right—
it's more like trying to keep everyone alive forever. Even the ones who
must die in the end. . . . A novelist is a doctor who sees only terminal cases,' Garp said. Young Whitcomb was so awed *that he wrote this
down*" (our emphases, 569–70). Returning to his apartment in one
of the Steering school's dormitories, Whitcomb "tried to write down
everything that had impressed him about Garp" (571), only to discover that his idol has been murdered. He nevertheless continues to
be dedicated to the Garps (he "would become as enchanted with
Helen as he was enchanted with the work of Garp" [579]), and ultimately writes the biography "years later, that the would-be biographers of Garp would all envy and despise" (570). Unlike other
cutthroat biographers waiting for Helen to die so "they could swoop
in on the remains of Garp" (580), Whitcomb becomes a close friend
of the family who "Helen would trust with the family and literary
record" (582), including, presumably, those things she refused access
to others: "his letters, the unfinished manuscript of *My Father's Illusions*, most of his journals and jottings" (580).

Sharing these private remains with Whitcomb because "she trusted
him to adore her husband perhaps even more uncritically than she
did" (582), Helen not only cooperates with his biographer, she actually contributes to shaping his work: "Whitcomb believed everything
that Helen told him—he believed every note that Garp left—or every
note that Helen *told* him Garp left" (582).

Through Helen's cooperation and revelations, Whitcomb ("who
loved Garp uncritically—in the manner of dogs and children") becomes the expert on Garp whose pronouncements are unchallenged
even by other members of the family. Asserting that Garp's last
words were indeed what Garp wanted them to be ("No matter what
my fucking last words were, please say they were these: 'I have always
known that the pursuit of excellence is a lethal habit' " [582]), Whitcomb persuades Duncan, Jenny Garp, and Ellen James that he is the
undisputed authority on these matters: " 'If Whitcomb said so, then
they were,' Duncan always said" (583).

The "official" biography ultimately written by Whitcomb would
be entitled *Lunacy and Sorrow: The Life and Art of T. S. Garp*, the first
part of which was Irving's original title for *The World According to
Garp*.[5] The narrator of Garp tells us that John Wolf "contributed

much effort to the book's careful making" (589) and that Helen "would read all but the last chapter . . . the chapter eulogizing her" (582).

It may not, therefore, be assuming too much to speculate that Whitcomb is, in fact, the unnamed, ostensibly omniscient narrator of *The World According to Garp* and that we are actually reading the so-called biography, *Lunacy and Sorrow.* For the narrator may indeed be playfully creating the illusion of distance and omniscience in order to suggest the Victorian mode at the same time he self-mockingly characterizes himself as "a monkish recluse all his life, which he spent in virtual hiding at the Steering School" (582) and, in a self-parody of the scholar, as an apparently sexless, powerless academic whose "voice would remain a stuttering, eager yodel; his hands would wring themselves forever" (582). Indispensable friend to the family (he even ensures that Helen is cremated and has the funeral and epitaph she requested), Whitcomb has sole access to letters, manuscripts, and Garp's sardonic notes, which are quoted hundreds of times in the novel, and to the friends, relatives, and associates who people Garp's world. Working with John Wolf and Duncan, Whitcomb even becomes the vehicle whereby *My Father's Illusions* is published "considerably posthumously" (590). His apparently reticent, reclusive nature is belied by the powerful position he establishes for himself while all other would-be biographers languish ("*It was a family matter—keeping Garp from the biographers,* wrote Ellen James" [583]). "Through an omniscient narrator," as Michael Priestley puts it, "Irving has imposed order and structure upon the 'lunacy and sorrow' of the world within his novel—just as Donald Whitcomb has in his biography of Garp, and as Garp has in his writing, which is actually the 'world according to Garp.' "[6]

Perhaps refusing to speculate on the potential of Whitcomb as narrator (the "fact" of which we can never be certain), Michael Priestley nevertheless comes close to making the identification:

The epilogue, "Life After Garp," is added for the purpose of " 'warning us about the future,' as T. S. Garp might have imagined it" (414). Why are these quotations and the epilogue included? One explanation is that Irving uses them to remind us of the unquestionable omniscience of the narrator, who is intended to be Garp's official biographer: he has created this world and he knows what is going to happen because the entire book exists in his mind. He began writing the book after Garp had died.[7]

Since we will be told that Whitcomb's book is the "official biography" (589), it is indeed tempting to consider Whitcomb as artist/narrator/biographer creating as much as chronicling the world according to Garp—an "omniscient" voice in the novelistic tradition, but a clever man in the very corporeal world that is Irving's. And perhaps Irving cues us again when he indirectly raises the issue of narrative perspective in the very section of the novel that deals most directly with Whitcomb's role: "[Helen] herself wrote several articles, which were respected in her field. One was called 'The Adventurer's Instinct in Narration.' It was a comparative study of the narrative technique of Joseph Conrad and Virginia Woolf" (580). Perhaps the "adventurer's instinct" is alive, well, and up to new tricks in *The World According to Garp*.[8]

"A Sophisticated Metafictional Investigation"

Given his repeated and apparently total disdain for fiction about fiction, John Irving might find Larry McCaffery's description of *Garp* the typical and, for Irving, reprehensible mutterings of the academic critic: "*Garp* may be, above all, a funny and poignant family saga, but it is also a sophisticated metafictional investigation into the writer's relationship to his work, the nature of art and the imagination; in addition it speaks to us forcefully about the dangers and hatreds lurking in our modern-day society, the mortality we all must face, and how art and love may assist man in dealing with death."[9]

Having created several important characters "who stand aghast at the new fiction,"[10] it is evident that Irving views the Barthian penchant for metafictional discourse and analysis as sounding the death knell for the novel as a lively artistic form: "Irving's fiction stubbornly sets out to breathe new life into the genre without actually acknowledging such a death."[11] At first glance, it would therefore seem reasonable, as Hugh Ruppersburg suggests, to view the subject of art as a secondary interest of Irving's and as a tertiary subject of *The World According to Garp*. "Though art is certainly an important part of Garp's life, it is crucial to the novel's meaning that [it] is only incidentally a theme. Had Garp been a fireman or a lawyer, his essential story would not be much changed."[12]

Had Garp been a fireman or a lawyer, however, *The World According to Garp* would be, among other things, a much shorter novel—a shorter novel which could not, as it does now, reveal directly the essence of Garp's vision through the fictions he creates and the fictions he describes. Indeed, had Garp been a fireman, we would lose not only the marvelous "Pension Grillparzer," "Vigilance," and the first chapter of *The World According to Bensenhaver,* we would lose: the letters to Mrs. Poole (one of which contains an instructional fable); the entire chapter "The Dog in the Alley, the Child in the Sky"; the summaries of Garp's novels, *Procrastination, Second Wind of the Cuckold,* and *The World According to Bensenhaver*; the projected plots of a three novel sequence, *My Father's Illusions, The Death of Vermont,* and *The Plot against the Giant*; and, we would certainly lose Whitcomb and the story of the biographers since, presumably, few would be interested in the life and death of a fireman, however heroic.

No matter how vociferously Irving and many of his characters reject the "new fiction," he and they never reject the metaphor of art and its relation to the life well lived; nor do they reject the artist who is, above all else, a man attempting to deal with the chaos that defines human experience. For *all* of Irving's protagonists are "artists" in one way or another, whether they are constructing journals, films, historical novels, fiction, illusions, or doctoring terminal cases. Their constructs establish order where none exists; their structures mitigate the awful pain of existence: "Like the village explainer . . . Irving resembles both the Victorian novelist ('dear reader') and the 'new novelist' who writes fiction about fiction. In each of his novels, he has imposed structure upon his fictional world; his characters, then, explain the structure, question its validity, and proceed to search for a new structure, a personal vision of their own."[13]

While both McCaffery and Priestley recognize how central the subject of art is to Irving's work, they also indirectly articulate how his treatment differs markedly from that of Gass, Pynchon, or Barth. McCaffery, for example, identifies art as one of two concurrent themes in *Garp*: "how art and love may assist man in dealing with death." Priestley, on the other hand, describes a balance in terms of traditional and contemporary approaches: "Irving resembles both 'the Victorian novelist' . . . and the 'new novelist' who writes fiction about fiction."

This blending of conventional, always vital human concerns and the "metafictional investigation" is achieved with extraordinary skill in *Garp* primarily because the aesthetic debate is dramatized through the character of Garp as artist: it is not reduced to abstraction or to the realm of theme qua theme as it frequently is in much contempo-

rary literature. For however much Barth's "Ambrose Mensch" represents a self-mocking parody of the artist in *Letters*, and however much
he playfully protests "But art! All this is not what all this is about!
(*What, then, Ambrose?*),"[14] Barth is often engaged in sophisticated aesthetic debate which eclipses and supersedes all other psychological
and emotional experience. As a result, Barth (among others) is frequently perceived as a profoundly more important writer than Irving,
whose own claim to serious aesthetic interests, is, by some critics,
simply ignored:

The negative response to John Barth's *Letters* (1979) is instructive and should
be juxtaposed to the acclamation afforded John Irving's *The World According
to Garp*. While very difficult to read and in many aspects a display of authorial self-indulgence, *Letters* is a significant cultural event. For it does what
literature is supposed to do, which is to probe new modes of perception,
however tedious the process. *Letters* must be given time to find its level.[15]

Irving—as well as Jillsy Sloper—would, to be sure, find it amusing that *Letters* is an apparently superior novel to *Garp* despite the fact
(or perhaps *due* to the fact?) that it is "very difficult to read," "tedious," and frequently represents "authorial self-indulgence." It is
perhaps also instructive that Barth himself apparently recognizes the
importance not only of serious aesthetic themes but the value of traditional forms as well, for he subtitles *Letters*: "An Old Time Epistolary
Novel By Seven Fictitious Drolls and Dreamers Each of Which Imagines Himself Actual." Irving might well have developed *Garp* as "An
Old Time Epistolary Novel" in which each narrator, each voice,
"imagines himself actual."

"Imagination . . . Came Harder Than Memory"

Our argument here is not, however, with Barth, the brilliant and
obvious successor to Joyce. Rather, it is with those who fail to see
that Irving—Dickens's distant heir—also does "what literature is
supposed to do" by probing "new modes of perception," perception
about life and art, and does so in unique ways in *Garp*. Irving presents products of Garp's literary output at key points in his artistic
career and embeds those examples in a richly textured story. Because
Garp is a writer, that story quite naturally focuses on interpretation

and discussion of his fiction. Thus, Irving successfully integrates "fiction about fiction" with powerful (and more traditional and universal) human struggles to live life meaningfully.

The first such substantive treatment of aesthetic themes occurs as young Garp grapples with what will be his initial short story, "The Pension Grillparzer." As a result of seeing several unusual people and a pathetic performing bear in one of his excursions around Vienna, Garp imagines a story that will somehow combine this "decrepit circus" (124) with "a close, interesting family" (122). While he finds it simple to create a "plot," he recognizes that the story must embody meaning and that "he did not have a scheme of things" (123). Aware that his mother's incessant outpourings at the typewriter reflect a need to deal almost exclusively with her personal past, Garp realizes that his story must be something quite different: "Imagination, he realized, came harder than memory" (124).

In order to stimulate his own imagination (and simultaneously develop a "scheme of things"), Garp does several things typical of aspiring writers and young intellectuals: he studies two other writers—one a sentimentalist and one a philosopher—both former inhabitants of Vienna, the city that is alleged to provide artistic inspiration. What Garp learns from the two is seminal to his budding vocation: comparing Franz Grillparzer's work with Dostoyevsky's, he learns that the difference between "serious writing" and "tearful trivia" "was not subject matter. The difference, Garp concluded, was intelligence and grace; the difference was art" (126); he learns from Marcus Aurelius the "subject of most serious writing" is "the life of a man" in which "his time is but a moment, his being an incessant flux, his sense a dim rushlight, his body a prey of worms, his soul an unquiet eddy, his fortune dark, his fame doubtful. In short, all that is body is as coursing waters, all that is of the soul as dreams and vapors" (126). Understanding that craft is more important than subject matter and that "the scheme of things" is that there is *no* "scheme of things" are critical lessons for Garp, lessons that, when combined with profound emotional experience, provide the foundation for his developing art and the basis for his maturing vision.

The story that ultimately results from these insights and experiences perfectly illustrates Garp's developing aesthetic and, by extension, Irving's. For "The Pension Grillparzer" is a superbly crafted story of an imagined series of meetings between "a close, interesting family" and an eccentric "decrepit circus" cum performing bear and assorted bizarre characters. It is a story whose "scheme of things" is the transience of life, the ubiquitousness of both the dream and reality of death, and man's overwhelming desire to transcend these realities through human compassion and creativity.

The last sentence of the story reflects the stoicism of Aurelius transmitted through a character who will be one of the many artist figures in both Garp's fiction (and in Irving's): "There was in her story the flatness one associates with a storyteller who is accepting of unhappy endings, as if her life and her companions had never been exotic to *her*—as if they had always been staging a ludicrous and doomed effort at reclassification" (180).

The "ludicrous and doomed effort at reclassification," while literally referring to the circus family's increasingly less successful attempts to achieve a higher rating for the shabby pension they manage, is a controlling metaphor in Garp's first story, in his life, and in his aesthetic: indeed, it comes to define his personal vision and ultimately to reflect Irving's. While the characters in Garp's fiction will forever be engaged in the optimistic pursuit of transcendent value and meaning, their "efforts at reclassification"—at imbuing life with structure, order, and meaning—will inevitably be doomed. But for these efforts, Garp will always find laughter and sympathy in the artistic act and will reflect those in the stuff of his art.

The next significant development in Garp's aesthetic occurs after he and Helen are married and he begins writing in earnest. His second novel, *Second Wind of the Cuckold*, is a thinly disguised roman à clef, the story of two couples who exchange partners and engage in a messy ménage à quatre (an obvious ironic reference to Irving's *The 158-Pound Marriage*). While each of the "characters" is in some way maimed, they are nevertheless recognizable as parodies of the Garps and Fletchers, a couple with whom the Garps briefly exchange sex and friendship.

Although Garp adamantly denies the novel's autobiographical nature, Helen remains unconvinced: "You have your own terms for what's fiction, and what's fact, but do you think other people know your system? It's all your *experience*—somehow, however much you make up, even if it's only an *imagined* experience" (227). The struggle to capture what is truly imagined rather than to reflect simply what one has personally experienced becomes a life-long artistic challenge for Garp, a challenge that will become even more profound as he suffers extraordinary pain and loss.

"A Truthful Contradiction"

Having now discovered the importance of craft, an existential world view that defines the "scheme of things," and the dangers of autobiographical fiction, Garp the artist will also have the opportunity to define and articulate, perhaps for the first time, his personal aesthetic—the qualities that mark his unique vision and art. Responding to an outraged reader, Mrs. Irene Poole of Findlay, Ohio, a woman who accuses him of failing to be sympathetic with human suffering, Garp explains his aesthetic:

> . . . *I have never understood why "serious" and "funny" are thought to be opposites. It is simply a truthful contradiction to me that people's problems are often funny and that the people are often and nonetheless sad.*
>
> *I am ashamed, however, that you think I am laughing at people, or making fun of them. I take people very seriously. People are all I take seriously, in fact. Therefore, I have nothing but sympathy for how people behave—and nothing but laughter to console them with.*
>
> *Laughter is my religion, Mrs. Poole.* (233)

And while he is totally unsuccessful persuading the intransigent and humorless Mrs. Poole of the sincerity and value of his perspective (she responds: "You must be a sick man" [236]), by virtue of this correspondence, Garp has etched an aesthetic against which he (and we) will now measure his future work.

Garp offers us the opportunity to take such a measure in due course, for, at this point in his life and artistic career, he is struggling unsuccessfully to create meaningful fiction. Having published two novels which sold poorly even though they received modestly enthusiastic reviews, he writes the short story "Vigilance" in an attempt simultaneously to break out "of his writing slump" (320) and to regain Helen's attention and affection, both of which he instinctively knows are elsewhere. The story is, however, a dull, self-indulgent exercise about a father chasing a careless man whose driving threatens children in a quiet suburban neighborhood—a story with few of the characteristics Garp himself has identified as manifestations of his aesthetic: " 'It's all one-liners. I mean, what *is* it? A self-parody? You're not old enough, and you haven't written enough, to start mocking yourself. It's self-serving, it's self-justifying; and it's not about anything except yourself, really. It's cute. . . . It's no "Grillparzer," certainly. . . . It isn't worth a *tenth* of that story,' Helen said" (333).

In addition to serving as a concrete measure of Garp's temporary artistic failures, "Vigilance" acts as a metaphor for the state of his personal life: like his marriage, the story lacks luster and imaginative energy. As he does in virtually all his novels, Irving here uses art to symbolize various states of emotional well-being and crisis: an artifact—whether actual (like a Bruegel painting) or created by him for metaphoric purposes—not only embodies experience in some important way, its shape and passion (or lack thereof) provide an objective correlative—a signpost—for the affective world of his characters at critical times in their lives.

Just so, "Vigilance" is the last thing Garp is to write before the horrible accident irrevocably wrenches his and Helen's life into a new pattern marked by almost exquisite suffering. Losing his younger son, dealing with the partial mutilation of Duncan and the painful and frustrating—both physical and psychic—injuries to himself and Helen, Garp is temporarily speechless in much more than the literal sense: "When he tried to write, only the deadliest subject rose up to greet him. He knew he had to forget it—not fondle it with his memory and exaggerate its awfulness with his art. . . . And so he did not write; he didn't even try" (388).

But, for Garp, the healing process inevitably manifests itself in the revitalization of his artistic imagination, and while Helen, sensing its awful potential, refuses, in advance, to read the book, Garp "began to write—gingerly, at first" (389). The product, a novel called *The World According to Bensenhaver*, will be the novel that assures Garp commercial success and financial independence: it will also represent the horrific receptacle "into which all his *other* feelings flew" (399): art as therapy.

Recognizing the symbiotic relationships between Garp's emotional state and his third novel, Gabriel Miller contends that:

The World According to Bensenhaver represents a complete surrender of purpose, a dramatic loss of creative voice as a result of his inability to feel or articulate properly the horror of his own experience. . . . Garp loses control of his art in a convulsive outpouring of his personal feelings of outrage, revulsion, and despair. . . . *The World According to Bensenhaver* is a graphic and lurid reflection of the violence in Garp's world, wherein the author's darkest fears are allowed free rein in a sensational tale of rape, murder, paranoia, and guilt.[16]

If we were presented only with a paraphrase of the novel, a paraphrase which does indeed reflect the characteristics he suggests,

Miller's reading of the function and quality of *The World According to Bensenhaver* would be accurate and fair to both Garp and Irving. We are, however, once again exposed directly to the thing itself in the form of the first chapter of the novel. And a careful reading of the chapter indicates that while it indeed represents a "graphic and lurid reflection of the violence in Garp's world," it in no way reflects either "a dramatic loss of creative voice," nor does it illustrate how "Garp loses control of his art." Quite the contrary, "The World According to Bensenhaver" represents how the artist harnesses and gives shape to inchoate feelings and creates structures that serve to exorcise his deepest fears and fantasies. For in this case, Irving invites us to engage in both quasi-Freudian and aesthetic analysis simultaneously: we can understand Garp the man through the direct evidence of Garp the artist as it is presented in the first chapter of his own novel.

The first thing Garp does when he conceives of this novel is to avoid "the main characters. . . . He concentrated instead on a detective, an outsider to the family. Garp knew what terror would lurk at the heart of his book, and perhaps for that reason he approached it through a character as distant from his personal anxiety as the police inspector is distant from the crime" (389). Literally using a police inspector as the primary sensibility through which the awful events of the story will be filtered and interpreted, Garp seems to create, almost by definition, an objective distance in the dominant consciousness, just as he did by creating a similar objectivity in the "I" narrator of "The Pension Grillparzer," a narrator who reveals his occupation only at the very end of the story: "Because I appeared to know so much about her past associates, she probably knew I was with the police" (178).[17]

Because police inspector Arden Bensenhaver's wife had herself been brutally raped and died by choking on her own vomit, however, his "distance" from the rape of Hope Standish is deceptive. While his behavior in handling the case is apparently "objective," his sympathy for the victim allows him to tell absurd lies and manipulate evidence to ensure that real justice is done. So, much like the narrator's father in "Pension Grillparzer," an inspector for the Austrian Tourist Bureau who, out of compassion, manipulates the rating system to favor the hapless managers of the Pension, Bensenhaver temporarily shields Hope Standish from further pain by making sure her killing of the rapist is unquestionably deemed an act of self defense: "In the world according to Bensenhaver, no trivial detail should make less of rape's outrage" (439).

In this story, as in "Pension Grillparzer," Garp has it both ways: his protagonists bring "objectivity" to painful experience, but that objectivity is softened and humanized by compassion which manipulates experience to create temporary reprieves—illusions of justice—in an inexorably violent, hostile, or, at best, indifferent universe.

In short, Garp is in control of his art when, as he does in the first chapter of *The World According to Bensenhaver* (and as he did in "The Pension Grillparzer"), he is able to create aesthetic distance from his material, even when that distance is mitigated by sympathy. At the same time he creates sympathetic distance through apparently "objective" characters such as Bensenhaver, he may simultaneously be exorcising personal agonies. For one might easily speculate that Hope Standish is a surrogate for Helen, forced into sex against her will by Oren Rath, a despicable and crude parody of Michael Milton, and that she kills him and is saved by the thoughtful Garp surrogate, Bensenhaver, police inspector as artist, as "the voice of God" (431), manipulating the gruesome world in the name of compassion: "She marveled how Bensenhaver could even turn her vomiting into a victory" (440), an act analogous to Garp's attempt to turn personal tragedy into healing reconciliation through art. Both of their "methods had been judged . . . unorthodox" (416).

It is no accident that two critical events occur concurrently in Garp's life: "Garp . . . finished *The World According to Bensenhaver* two weeks before Helen delivered, with Jenny's help, their third child—a daughter" (443). For, in the world according to Irving, art alone does not provide the means to live life fully. As McCaffery notes: "art and love may assist man in dealing with death," and, in this case, Garp's love for Helen, and its issue, represents a parallel experience to the creation of his third novel; both events allow Garp temporarily to transcend "the incessant flux" of life.

The notoriety of *Bensenhaver* is, however, painful to Garp because the novel is marketed and sold by exploiting the Garps' personal tragedy. Objecting to his publisher's method and reinforcing his commitment to acts of imagination rather than to art as autobiography, Garp reasserts his aesthetic, an aesthetic that will shape the short artistic career he has yet to live: "Fiction has to be better made than life. . . . The only reason for something to happen in a novel is that it's the perfect thing to have happen at the time. . . . Tell me *any*thing that's ever happened to you . . . and I can improve upon the story; I can make the details better than they were" (457).

There is no question that all three stories with which we are presented are designed to reflect Garp's maturing aesthetic purpose and vision and to be judged against that aesthetic. "I think they were the most ambitious things I've ever written," Irving has said. "I would never have written those kinds of things if I hadn't been doing them for Garp."[18] By his own indirect admission then, *The World According to Garp* is finally Irving's "metafictional investigation," but one that humanizes fully the artistic act and yokes it directly to the struggle to live meaningfully.

Tongues and Penises

Much as the writing of a novel and the birth of a child represent analogous creative acts that embody the ultimately affirmative nature of Garp's world and Irving's vision, a parallel set of images reinforces these emphases by providing a symbolic counterpoint to the primary metaphors of art and love in *The World According to Garp*. Multiple allusions to language and sexuality texture the novel and are repeatedly conveyed through a variety of situations that literally or figuratively incorporate tongues and penises as symbolic devices: "Language and sex are related in that both are potentially creative, connective forces whose uses, however, must be tempered with some constructive restraint; both may become powerful divisive influences when misused or abused."[19]

From the very outset of the novel, linguistic and sexual acts are juxtaposed in various symbolic relationships. Because both language and sex have the considerable potential either to capture and aggrandize the life force, or, conversely, to pervert or destroy that positive force, Irving creates multiple patterns in which the two intermingle or coalesce. Beginning the novel with a joke about Peter Bent Hospital—a joke that will later assume grim connotations—Irving adumbrates his serious intentions with crude humor: "It's worse than *bent* . . . I think Molly bit it *off*" (7).

The joke creates an ironic context for several key events in the novel and for Jenny's experience at Boston Mercy Hospital, including her resolve to become a mother; and the ideal candidate for father soon presents himself. Bereft of language because of his extensive battle wounds ("she knew he was dying. He had just one vowel and one consonant left" [27]), Technical Sergeant Garp is nevertheless very much alive sexually: "Under the sheet it smelled like a greenhouse in

almost unbearable pain. After he is ironically struck speechless by the accident that kills Walt, for example, Garp, who "had much to say that was immediate—and no way to say it" (377), at first misuses his prodigious way with words by writing vicious notes to Helen referring to Michael Milton's severed penis: *"Three quarters is not enough"* (380).[21] And while he has the common sense to destroy such notes before inflicting them on the already suffering Helen, Garp is slow to forgive the consequences of other people's lust, guilty of sexual indulgence though he has repeatedly been himself.

Unlike Helen, who *could* talk but "said little; she did not have pages and pages to say" (378), Garp's human problem with language is replicated by his problem as an artist; and it is only when he solves the human dilemma by extending Helen forgiveness that his art can flow again.

But that art, as we have shown, is full of fearful experience. A story of perverse sexuality and violence, "The World According to Bensenhaver" reverberates with the symbols of that perversity. Originally planning to rape Hope in the Standish home, Oren Rath threatens her baby: "You want to talk about choking? I'll cut his pecker off and stuff it down his throat—if you want to talk about choking" (402). Desperately attempting to extricate herself from Rath's grasp, Hope herself has a parallel fantasy: "Could I bite the damn thing off? she wondered" (412). Even the mutilation theme in the story is subject to black comedy, for Bensenhaver threatens the Rath brothers with a nonexistent penalty: *"Any* sexual crime . . . is now punishable by castration . . . we can castrate you" (423). And finally, in refusing to forgive Rath merely because he is a minor, Bensenhaver summarizes his philosophy regarding the perpetrators of rape: "If he's old enough to get a hard-on . . . he's old enough to have it cut off" (427).

Garp's obsession with penis mutilation and castration is, of course, a direct reflection of the horrors of the accident. But it is only an emotionally heightened variation of his life-long personal struggle with the fact of lust and the relationship of lust to manhood and self-identity. Because Jenny is such a sexless creature herself (whose clinical, implicitly judgmental queries of the adolescent Garp make him uncomfortably self-conscious), Garp finds his natural sexual urges developing in a less than receptive climate. And although he becomes a remarkably well-adjusted adult, he never forgets his mother's concerns or underrates the literal or psychic havoc lust can engender: "he had outgrown baby-sitters. But lust itself? Ah, well. Jenny Fields had fingered a problem at the heart of her son's heart" (217).

None of his concern with the ravages of lust or of misused sexuality makes Garp—or, by extension, Irving—a conventional moralist in any way. On the contrary, Garp has the most tolerant of attitudes toward those who seek love by whatever means or in whatever form, as his affection for Roberta Muldoon readily attests. What Garp needs to discover—before he dies—is that he has a singular commitment to a woman and family and that with Helen "he shared . . . the vulnerability of conjugal love" (522). "Garp was happy with Helen. He wasn't unfaithful to her, anymore; that thought seldom occurred to him. . . . Enough of his life had been influenced by lust" (525).

Analogously, he tries to bring language under control, just as the real Ellen James does, by shaping it into art. And though he has occasional lapses (he publishes a poem about condoms: "Garp felt his life was marred by condoms—man's device to spare himself and others the consequences of his lust" [553]), his art returns to products of his imagination rather than of his memory: "He was working on what he called his 'father book' . . . the novel to be called *My Father's Illusions*. Because he was inventing a father, Garp felt more in touch with the spirit of pure imagination that he felt had kindled 'The Pension Grillparzer' " (563).

Unfortunately, the loveless and speechless neither forget nor forgive Garp's previous excesses with sex or language; the newly self-mutilated Ellen Jamesian, Pooh Percy, murders him, inarticulately and ineffectually conveying her obscene message: " 'Igs!' she screamed. 'Ucking igs!' " (574). Death comes as "no stranger," but as the antithesis of art and life.

"People Are All I Take Seriously"

The fact that Irving is indeed a writer who explores aesthetic themes in his fiction in no way diminishes the emotional or psychological power of the human drama in which he invests his primary creative energies. For while it is critical to *The World According to Garp* that Garp is an artist, it is even more critical that he is a man grappling with fundamentally human problems—problems that, though universal, also have particular relevance to contemporary life as Irving sees it: violent, cacophonous, dehumanizing. And, in the face of those realities, certain values emerge as salvaging: family is paramount; personal commitments are essential; traditional sexual roles can be transformed into creative androgynous wholes; and, affirmation is not only possible, it is a necessary condition for living in a world where there are no happy endings.

Just as Garp saw no contradiction in taking people seriously while having "nothing but laughter to console them with" (233), so Irving's mode reflects the paradox of the comic-tragic vision. As Iowa Bob says in *The Hotel New Hampshire*: "Death is horrible, final, and frequently premature." Like Win Berry, Irving asks with his fiction: "So what?"

The World According to Garp is an unusual and brilliant book because, perhaps more effectively than most other post–World War II novels, it integrates a comic-tragic worldview characterized by "pretty desperate laughter" (233) with a traditional family saga told in the unforgettable manner of a narrator sure of his materials, affections, and values. It is also a unique novel because it manages to link in vital and lively ways timeless literary themes: how a human being can live, love, and affirm the positive values of experience. The novel accomplishes these things at the same time its energy and humor entertain, rather than instruct, us.

John Irving is bullish on the subject of the legitimacy of art as entertainment. Indeed, he raises the debate to an issue of principles: "Art has an *aesthetic* responsibility to be entertaining. The writer's responsibility is to take hard stuff and make it as accessible as the stuff can be made. Art and entertainment aren't contradictions."[22]

Like Garp, Irving is continuously engaged in transforming experience into art that is accessible, which will "reclassify" the world as we know it and enrich our lives. That the effort is ultimately "doomed" is inconsequential. His own "father book," *The Hotel New Hampshire*, will attempt that reclassification in the mode of the fairy tale, another literary permutation in the world according to Irving.

Chapter Six
The Hotel New Hampshire:
"So We Dream On"

Looking back in 1981, Irving admitted that he was "most pleased with *The Hotel New Hampshire* of the five books so far, in that, when I say it's the most fairy tale to me and I'm therefore the most pleased with it, what I mean is that it seems to me the most complete unto itself—that is, it is the most of itself an entered and then left world. You enter it . . . and while you're in it, *its* rules apply, yours don't."[1] By design and structure, Irving's fifth novel, *The Hotel New Hampshire*, is a modern fairy tale. And, as Gabriel Miller suggests in his very perceptive (if occasionally forced) analysis of the novel—an analysis based on Bruno Bettelheim's paradigmatic discussion of fairy tales in *The Uses of Enchantment*[2]—the power of *The Hotel New Hampshire* emanates from its evocation of dream, magic, and sacred literary symbols and motifs. Irving's fifth novel does indeed embody a world "complete unto itself," and in so doing represents a new phase in the writer's literary development, a phase adumbrated in *The World According to Garp* but not fully entered until *Hotel*.

A fairy tale is, however, only one species of the generic type known as romance. And though Miller's convincing explication of *The Hotel New Hampshire* as fairy tale generously enriches our critical insight into this unusual novel, an even more complete understanding of Irving's method and achievement can be gained by viewing the novel in the larger context of the American version of the romantic tradition. For with this novel Irving secures his identity as fabulist and maker of modern myth in the manner, if not the level of excellence, of his American literary predecessors from Hawthorne through Faulkner. And, however much *The Hotel New Hampshire* fails to replicate the power and complexity of *Garp*, it nevertheless represents a bold attempt to cast contemporary human experience in psychologically meaningful, symbolic terms that belong to the quintessentially

American dream, and hence, the romantic tradition much as Richard
Chase defines it:

the word [*romance*] must signify, besides the more obvious qualities of the
picturesque and the heroic, an assumed freedom from the ordinary novelistic
requirements of verisimilitude, development, and continuity; a tendency toward melodrama and idyl; a more or less formal abstractness and, on the
other hand, a tendency to plunge into the underside of consciousness; a willingness to abandon moral questions or to ignore the spectacle of man in society, or to consider these things only indirectly or abstractly.[3]

The vehicle that Irving employs to signal his kinship with the tradition of the romance and to provide a literary objective correlative
and structural metaphor is *The Great Gatsby*. Indeed, incremental references to, and various analogues from, *The Great Gatsby* are inter-
woven into the fabric of *The Hotel New Hampshire* in an increasingly
ironic, yet ultimately serious way. The novel's refrain—"So we dream
on"—becomes both the definition of the story John Berry tells ‾ ‾
the consciously evoked key to placing *The Hotel New Hampshire*
squarely in the American literary tradition.

On the surface, of course, *The Hotel New Hampshire* bears little re-
semblance to Fitzgerald's great novel and even less to the classic
American romance-novel. Its Dickensian texture, comic-satiric tone,
and melodramatic action are more nearly the qualities of "X-rated
soap opera" (Garp's characterization of his third novel, *The World According to Bensenhaver* [*Garp* 447]) than they are similar to the poetics
of idyll so often manifest in romance. But Irving seems to be attempting a new fusion, a new construct which combines recognizable
elements of soap opera with classic American romantic themes and
psychological experiences; in so doing he clearly demonstrates the
principle of reciprocity which T. S. Eliot years ago defined as the
fruitful relationships between "tradition and the individual talent."

Five Hotels

The twelve chapters of the novel are asymmetrically organized
around the five hotels (not the *three* so many critics identify) that
define the actual or symbolic homes of the Winslow Berry family.

Living only briefly in a traditional family domicile belonging to his in-laws, Win Berry, preeminent dreamer and contemporary Gatsby figure, imaginatively engenders what will become his rapidly growing family at the shabby genteel pre–World War II resort hotel, the Arbuthnot-by-the-Sea. Constantly seeking the dream, he then moves them, dwindling in numbers though they too quickly become, through a succession of four other hotels, three of which will be known as the first, second, and last Hotels New Hampshire. (The fourth hotel, New York's Stanhope, provides a transition between the second and third Hotels New Hampshire and acts as a temporary symbolic passage between decadent Europe and the final return to the pristine New England coast.)

In addition to the structural pattern of clustering chapters around hotels which become either symbolic or actual homes, a larger, archetypal structure and movement is simultaneously developed. According to Chase, this movement typifies patterns in American romance-novels that integrate or subsume the essence of folklore: "the drama of light and dark . . . life and death, good and evil, male and female, angel and demon, God and Satan, summer and winter," patterns "widespread if not universal in folklore."[4] In *The Hotel New Hampshire*, this archetypal movement takes the primary form of a dramatic as well as geographic shift in landscape from America to Vienna back to America, wherein Vienna represents the dark, the decadent, the incorrigible but necessary interruption of innocence by bleak experience. As Irving himself says, "The reason they go to Vienna is that that's what happens when you grow up: you go to a foreign country."[5] Or, as Joseph Campbell would have it, the journey represents the classic "rites of passage": separation, initiation, return.[6]

Within what, therefore, seems a classic light-dark-light, America-Europe-America scheme contrapuntally organized around five hotels is a far more cluttered, frenetic, and character-filled plot than might be anticipated. Employing something like the Dickensian mode of creating archetypal structures to organize a fictional world teeming with characters (many of whom are abstractions or two-dimensional, virtually emblematic figures or psychological types), Irving develops a hermetic universe of often bizarre, sometimes mutilated, frequently amoral or immoral characters whose actions inevitably impinge upon or work to sabotage the essentially wholesome, albeit eccentric, domestic world of the Berry family.

"An X-Rated Fairy Tale"

The actual narrative begins with a story, itself a kind of miniature fairy tale which signals the fundamental mode of the novel. Narrated entirely by John Berry, the third and middle child of Win and Mary Berry, the novel begins with a family reenactment of the past and Mary and Win's romantic union at the Arbuthnot-by-the-Sea, a reenactment that has the tonality and all the elements of the romantic idyll: "You imagine the story better than I remember it" (2).

Middle-class children of the also shabby and genteel town of Dairy, New Hampshire (whose economic and social focus is two single-sex and second rate prep schools), Mary and Win grow up together with no relationship except common birth years, her family-imposed desire to marry a Harvard man, and his vague yearning to *be* a Harvard man. They come together quite by chance when they are working as staff in the summer of 1939 at the almost otherworldly Arbuthnot-by-the-Sea resort hotel—a hotel that will be transformed from the shabby to the elegant by a love-induced act of imagination.

Catering to a middle-class New England version of a Gatsby-like crowd, the hotel has a mysterious and romantic owner who glides to and from his business in a white sloop and who employs a Viennese Jew, aptly named Freud, whose sole claim to fame is his pathetic but amusing trained bear named State O' Maine, later to be renamed, Earl.

As Miller rightly suggests, Freud plays the metaphorically multi-faceted role of wizard, sexual consciousness, and historical presence which all have great significance for the incipient lovers Win and Mary.[7] Planting the dream of theatrical success in Win's imagination and selling him the bear and motorcycle to activate the dream journey, Freud also acts as priest (or rabbi) to Win and Mary by first articulating and then sanctioning their love; paradoxically, he also indirectly prophesies the dream's inevitable doom by exacting Mary's promise to forgive Win for sins or mistakes not yet committed.

That Freud is also a Viennese Jew about to reenter Europe on the eve of the *Anschluss* is particularly significant; for however insulated from social and political reality the Berrys are (as are most of Irving's characters, particularly the later ones whose world is almost exclusively defined by domestic relationships), they are also very much a part of a world bracketed by the unprecedented horrors of the Holocaust on the one hand, and the violent, often anarchistic milieu of the contemporary scene on the other. Thus, Freud's presence at the onset of "my father's illusions" and his literal or symbolic re-emergence at several other key points in the novel establishes a pattern of the dream revived at precisely the moments it seems most likely to falter.

Marrying Mary Bates and promptly impregnating her, Win (who will soon be referred to simply as "Father") travels across the country-side with Earl playing seedy hotels, casinos, and resorts attempting to earn enough money to attend Harvard. Returning between stints only long enough to make Mary pregnant twice more, he begins work at Harvard, soon to recognize the inevitability of serving in World War II. Joining the army and having the good fortune to escape active combat, he returns from Europe, fathers a fourth child, graduates from Harvard and begins teaching English and coaching at the Dairy School where his father, "Iowa Bob," coaches football and where his father-in-law once taught Latin.

Yoked into a solidly domestic and routine life and missing the adventure of the past, Win takes the family to Maine to revitalize the dream evoked by the Arbuthnot-by-the-Sea; much to their dismay, however, they find the resort in ruins and permanently "closed for the season" (43). Shocked by the waste of "what it *could* have been" (44), Father is dealt an even more severe blow when Earl is accidentally shot by a local boy on the very dockside where Win previously took him fishing.

The romance engendered in Maine—the idyll around which Win Berry built his illusions—is apparently totally destroyed on that autumn day in 1946. And John the narrator, only four at the time, believes his father's devastation to be his "first memory of life itself—as opposed to what I was *told* happened, as opposed to the pictures other people have painted" (46). Here, at the end of chapter one, a microcosm of the archetypal enactment of the passage from innocence to experience (for both Father *and* son) seems to be complete. But Irving's version of the American dream has many transformations yet to be realized.

All the threads of the novel's tapestry are introduced in chapter 1 of *The Hotel New Hampshire*. Like classic romance or myth, the patterns of human experience are over and over embodied in natural and experiential cycles which end in death—the death of people, bears, and dreams. But Irving is no writer of pure tragedy and Win Berry and many of his family are survivors—displaying what is a form of heroism in Irving—if not all dreamers. Enter the dream endlessly revisited and the first Hotel New Hampshire.

Chapters 2–7 of the novel represent the longest sustained sequence in John's narrative and its most idyllic, if frequently troubled moments. Soon to be the complete family of Father, Mother, Frank (born 1940), Franny (1941), John (1942), Lilly (ca. 1946), Egg (ca. 1949), paternal grandfather Iowa Bob, and the flatulent Sorrow (a hapless black Labrador retriever—first surrogate for Earl the bear), the Berrys return to "normal" life in Dairy only to have thrust upon them the reincarnation of Win's dream. Spying the now abandoned Thompson Female Seminary, Father once again seizes the opportunity imaginatively to make a silk purse from a sow's ear: "In the darkness, where the imagination is never impeded, my father felt the name of his future hotel, and our future, coming to him" (69).

The sacrifices that must be made by all members of the Berry family to create the first Hotel New Hampshire combine an amusing set of physical accommodations (such as adapting to undersize bathroom fixtures—the "outhouse for elves"—and desks and chairs screwed down to the floor of what will become the restaurant) and a series of emotionally wrenching adjustments: Mother's family home is sold in order to renovate the old female seminary and the Berry family is dislocated and forced to live among eccentric staff and transient guests with all the attendant lack of privacy and inconveniences. But Father thinks of these sacrifices as "details" while John recognizes that "the first of my father's illusions was that bears could survive the life lived by human beings, and the second was that human beings could survive a life led in hotels" (70).

While the Berry family spends only four years (1953–57) conceiving of, developing, and living in the first Hotel New Hampshire, these years represent the critical maturation and initiation period for the three oldest children. In this relatively short but symbolically and psychologically critical period, Frank discovers and articulates his homosexuality, Franny is brutally gang raped and partially avenged by Junior Jones, leader of a vigilante gang of black athletes, John is initiated into sex and other aspects of traditional manhood. They all discover the lively sexuality of their parents; John and Franny recognize their affection for each other as dangerously close to incestuous; Sorrow dies; Iowa Bob is literally frightened to death by a crudely "resurrected" Sorrow; Lilly is diagnosed as being afflicted with dwarfism;

the hotel dies a slow economic death; and Father rediscovers Freud and dreams of another, more exotic version of the Hotel New Hampshire in Vienna. And, as if these extreme versions of the experience of adolescence were not sufficiently extensive and wrenching in themselves, Mother and Egg (along with the reincarnated figure of Sorrow) both die in a plane crash as they follow the rest of the family to Father's next illusory hotel.

"The Commercial Possibilities of a Simple Ideal"

The sequence in Vienna, comprising three chapters (8–10) and seven years (1957–64), moves the Berry family and the reader not only from the first to the second Hotel New Hampshire but from the relatively pristine world of New England (albeit a world fraught with Irvingesque experiences of gratuitous violence and untimely death) to the utterly incorrigible realm of fin de siècle Vienna, a city in the last stages of spiritual, political, and cultural entropy. If the traumas of adolescent human experience are metaphorically centered in the Halloween nightmare of Dairy, New Hampshire, the more profound horrors of adult experience are symbolically embodied in the Walpurgisnacht that is at the heart of post–World War II Vienna and in the clientele of this, the third, hotel.

Nothing in Vienna is what the family anticipated or of what Father dreamed. Freud has been blinded by Nazi terrorism, his female "bear" (a second Earl surrogate) is a woman hiding in a costume, another victim of brutal rape, and the Gasthaus Freud is not merely a shabby hotel, it is emblematic of a decadent culture which has no potential, at least for New England dreamers: "the pink, bovine nudes fallen in flowers of light (on the clashing floral wallpaper) . . . and the easy chair with its stuffing exploding (like the bombs to be imagined under all the debris in the outer districts) . . . and the one reading lamp too dim to dream by" (240).

The permanent residents of the hotel are a group of prostitutes and an enclave of radical terrorists euphemistically incognito as political intellectuals. John recognizes in these two groups more similarities than differences: "They both believed in the commercial possibilities of a simple ideal: they both believed they could, one day, be 'free.' They both thought that their own bodies were objects easily sacrificed for a cause (and easily restored, or replaced, after the hardship of the

sacrifice). Even their names were similar—if for different reasons"
(247–48). It is precisely the "commercial possibilities of a simple
ideal" that will define the ironies and ambiguities of Win's dream.
We are reminded here of Sherwood Anderson in such stories as "The
Egg," where we find a similar nexus of capitalistic hope and love in
the economic idealism of the father and the growing understanding
of the narrator son. This commercial ideal will determine the Berry
family's grotesque experience in Vienna and the meaning of that experience will once again be a shaping force in their lives and will thwart
the dream.

For the whores have no hearts of gold and the intellectuals are
mindless pornographers (both literally and figuratively), intent on
blowing up the Vienna State Opera House and the entire first district
because "it was all decadent. . . . It was full of disgust. They would
litter the Ringstrasse with *art*-lovers, with old-fashioned idealists silly
and irrelevant enough to like *opera*. They would make some point or
other by this kind of everything-bombing" (312).

John is alerted to the plot by one of the few sympathetic Viennese
figures we meet (other than Freud): a troubled young radical named
Fehlgeburt, astute student of American literature who reveals their
plan, simultaneously insists on John's initiating her sexually, and
then promptly commits suicide in despair over the loveless, valueless
world to which she has committed herself. Devastated by the experience, John turns once more quite literally to the bosom of his family
(drawing closer yet to Franny and incest), recognizing another catas-
trophe is about to smash his father's latest illusion.

While John has been flirting with both the radicals *and* the prostitutes, Franny has been trying to come to terms with the rape in her
past and her lingering and almost perverse attraction to the rapist and
to Ernst, the "idea man" (and literal pornographer) of the radical
group. In the meantime, Susie the bear, suppressing her own identity
(and hence psychic difficulties), but righteously criticizing Franny's
inability to hate her attacker, becomes Franny's temporary lover, an
apparently therapeutic experience for them both (seen by Irving, it
would appear, as a possible transitional process).

That all this melodramatic inversion of healthy human relationships is engendered in the second Hotel New Hampshire is hardly
part of Win Berry's plan; but, until he is forced to take an active role
in preventing the anarchists' mindless plot from destroying his dream
utterly, Father is mostly oblivious to the realities of a world out of

control. He becomes a "hero," however, when he kills Ernst with a Louisville Slugger (one version of the classic American dream symbol) just as Freud sacrifices his own life to neutralize the bomb. Father is ironically blinded in the ensuing explosion precisely at the same moment John squeezes one of the terrorists to death, thus discovering his own awful capacity to kill.

Having lost Freud (who Miller characterizes as a "supernatural helper"), Father is ready to quit the scene of the decimated second Hotel New Hampshire and take advantage of the family's newly acquired wealth. Since they "murdered the terrorists in [their] good old American family kind of way" (361), the status of heroes has been bestowed upon the Berrys. As a result, Frank, having evolved into a shrewd businessman, is able to command an exorbitant fee for the talented Lilly's novel *Trying to Grow*—a novel she has been painstakingly writing while other members of the family cavort with whores and political pornographers. "Dream on, Daddy," Lilly says, and the family moves temporarily to New York and their fourth hotel, the historic Stanhope.

". . . The *Last* One—I Promise You"

While in New York, John and Franny find their reciprocal affections impossible to repress any longer. Understanding the need to exorcise once and for all the unhealthy passion that binds them to each other and, equally destructive, to an endless childhood, Franny and John deliberately exhaust themselves making endless love. And the experience is curative: "the pain would convince us both that awaiting us in this particular pursuit of each other was our certain self-destruction" (377).

Free to live an independent adult life now, Franny must still transcend her lingering and perverse attachment to Chipper Dove, the man who, as a student, had raped her nine years before. Reconstituting their friendship with Susie and several of her rape victim friends, and without Father's knowledge, the Berry children construct a byzantine plot to avenge Franny and totally humiliate Chipper Dove. In a grotesque play-within-a-play sequence, they take their bizarre revenge but with little satisfaction: "Whatever we had done, it would never be as awful as what he had done to Franny—and if it *had* been as awful, it would have been too much" (403).

Dissatisfied living in New York, blind Father dreams on, this time about the Arbuthnot-by-the-Sea which he wishes to buy and restore: "It's the *last* one—I promise you" (409). Visiting old Arbuthnot, the owner, and once mysterious man in the white dinner jacket, Frank and John discover the nature of the reality; he is a vicious anti-Semite and wholly selfish capitalist who, on his deathbed, sells the old ruin "for a song" and assumes he has the last laugh.

After purchasing what Father will call the third Hotel New Hampshire, John commits himself to help Win Berry realize his dream again. "A joke is also the fulfillment of a wish. I had a joke to play on Father. And I have been playing it, now, for more than fifteen years" (414). Restoring the grounds and the interior, John creates the complete illusion that Father is the proprietor of a first class family hotel and ultimately peoples it with victims of rape and abuse who Father unknowingly nourishes through their recuperation. As Susie says: "And that's how you should treat a rape victim . . . they are holy, and you treat them as a great hotel treats every guest" (441).

The holiness of Susie is also made manifest as she becomes first John's lover and then his wife. Having both their love for Fanny and their "vision of Freud in common" (438), John and Susie have a "marriage made in heaven" (438) which is completed by their plans to adopt now famous actress Franny's baby, the issue of her marriage to Junior Jones, ex-football player and avenger turned lawyer.

Although during this otherwise idyllic period Lilly commits suicide in her despair over not being able to write the classic American novel, the remainder of the family flourishes in and around the placid third Hotel New Hampshire.

The fairy tale is complete: "So we dream on. Thus we invent our lives. . . . We invent what we love, and what we fear. . . . We dream on and on: the best hotel, the perfect family, the resort life. And our dreams escape us almost as vividly as we imagine them" (449). The thoroughly bogus hotel has become, in its own way, a real hotel. For Win Berry directly, and for his loyal children in another sense, a house is not a hotel. For the true hotel, at least the symbolic one, is a fully human dwelling, a place where kindness, tolerance, nurturing, and love—in short the conditions of the true family—can be realized. Such the third Hotel New Hampshire has become. Our dreams escape us, but they have, momentarily, their fruition. In romance, that moment may, on rare occasions, be frozen forever.

"The Green Light, the Orgiastic Future"

In one of his several moments of almost uncanny insight into the realities of life and into his son, Win's, incorrigibly romantic nature, Iowa Bob characterizes the essential vision of the dreamer: " 'The *future* again!' said Iowa Bob. 'He *lives* in the future!' " (59).

One of the central paradoxes at the heart of romance is, of course, how closely the dream of the future is inextricably bound to the imaginative re-creation of the past: "When the present offers nothing commensurate with man's capacity for wonder, the romantic credo is the belief—Gatsby's belief—in the ability to repeat the disembodied past."[8] It is perhaps also true that romantic dreamers such as Win Berry and Jay Gatsby do not, by definition, recognize the paradoxical nature of their own visions nor are they constitutionally capable of evaluating experience in any "objective" or "rational" sense.

Therefore, while it is clear that Jay Gatsby provides the energy for and is the focus of Fitzgerald's remarkable novel, it is also clear that he could not tell his own story. For Gatsby's understanding of his own experience and its significance is either limited or nonexistent; only a character like Nick Carraway—essentially more conservative and less given to a capacity for wonder—can objectify Gatsby's experience, place it in an existential context, and imbue it with meaning. Gatsby's experience and dream are ultimately misguided and doomed from the outset: "he can be made great only through reconstituting interpretation, reordering art."[9] Another way of understanding this fact is to recognize that Gatsby's experience and vision can only be realized in a romance, not in a novel where the laws of social and psychological validity subordinate the meaning and value of symbol and myth.

Likewise, although Win Berry is, in many ways, the ostensible focus of *The Hotel New Hampshire*, his dreams and experiences also require imaginative arrangement and implicit interpretation, and John Berry, "the middle child, and the least opinionated" (2) becomes Irving's Nick Carraway. However dissimilar John's relationship to his father seems compared with Nick's "objective" relationship to Gatsby, they both have or develop an emotional stake in the well-being and success of the dreams they describe. Moreover, like Nick, who ultimately manipulates situations and actually panders for Gatsby, John directly participates in his father's illusions by reinforcing them—by literally twice creating the mechanisms that foster the on-going life and liveliness of the dream when it would otherwise die. And John links his personal participation to his role as an artist: "to set the record straight or nearly straight" (2). Having intercepted a letter from Freud to Father, John speculates: "Like any storyteller, I had the power to end the story, and I could have. But I didn't destroy Freud's letter; I gave it to Father, while the vision of the man in the white dinner jacket was still upon him. I handed over Freud's let-ter—like any storyteller, knowing (more or less) where we would all be going" (192).

Thus, while Father is the dreamer and his dreams become the rai-son d'être for every move the otherwise "screwed down . . . for *life*" (132) Berry family will make, John is the artist manipulator, alter-nately creating and rendering as story the experiences that are the consequences of his father's dreams. And John quite self-consciously yokes together the role he later chooses to play and the artistic tradi-tion from which the role emanates: "But in my first few years of look-ing after Father at the third Hotel New Hampshire, that is rather what I felt like much of the time: a kind of weight-lifting maiden aunt. With a degree in American literature from Vienna, I could do worse than become the caretaker of my father's illusions" (417). In fact, John becomes not merely a caretaker of those illusions, but the proprietor and manager of them, an artist *in* life as well as *of* life.

But it is Lilly who first makes the explicit connection between the Berry family experience and *The Great Gatsby*. Overwhelmed by the beauty and power of the ending of Fitzgerald's novel (as the doomed Fehlgeburt excitedly reads it to the Berry children), Lilly blurts out her perception and sorrow: "it was *Father* she was crying for. 'Father is a *Gatsby*,' she cried. 'He *is*! I know he is!' " (257). Moreover, Lilly extends the analogy further, associating Father and Gatsby with the archetypal pursuit of the American dream:

It's the man in the white dinner jacket, it's Father, he's a Gatsby. "It eluded us then, but that's no matter—" Lilly quoted to us. "Don't you *see?*" she shrieked. "There's always going to be an *It*—and *It* is going to elude us, every time. It's going to *always* get away," Lilly said. "And Father's not go-ing to stop," she said. "He's going to keep going after it, and it's always going to get away. Oh, damn it!" she howled, stamping her little foot. "Damn it! Damn it!" (257)

Lilly recognizes here what has always been an unspoken family conviction: that Win Berry, like Gatsby, will forever pursue a dream, an "It," that is unattainable. In quoting the "It eluded us then" line from the end of Fitzgerald's novel, Lilly has a kind of epiphany which connects her father not only to the fictional character of Gatsby, but to the irrevocably lost American dream. For Nick Carraway's perception that "it eluded us then" refers to the "transitory enchanted moment" when the Dutch sailors beheld the "fresh, green breast of the new world" and dreamed of an Eden revisited: "face to face for the last time in history with something commensurate to [their] capacity for wonder."[10] Lilly's frustration, therefore, is not simply her recognition of the futility of her father's quest, but reflects her insight into a fundamentally mythic paradox, an American tragedy: "the work of the imagination in the New World" juxtaposed against "its failure to discover an objective for the romantic capacity."[11] And while Father is not like Gatsby—ultimately both an amoral and a tragic figure— he is not only because he is saved from annihilation or irreconcilable disappointment and failure by a mere "trick"—a magical illusion that he has indeed realized the dream: an illusion created and sustained by John Berry, self-described "realist": "I was just a realist in a family of dreamers, large and small. I knew I *couldn't* grow. I knew I would never really grow up; I knew my childhood would never leave me, and I would never be quite adult enough—quite responsible enough—for the world. The goddamm *Welt*, as Frank would say. I couldn't change enough, and I knew it" (259).

This self-effacing and self-protective assessment of his role as narrator and essentially reactive player in the Win and Franny Berry story is articulated at the very beginning of the novel ("the middle child, and the least opinionated") and is repeated at several key points in the novel, culminating in the "caretaker of my father's illusions" image. Through these and other echoes, Irving wishes to evoke the memory of Nick Carraway, also an ostensibly modest narrator, "rather literary in college," "inclined to reserve all judgments," and self-proclaimed keeper of conservative and unromantic values. "I am one of the few honest people that I have ever known" (60).

As we discover, however, both narrators are at least as much participants as observers; they are also involved, to one degree or another, in actually manipulating (as Arden Bensenhaver was)—even lying about—the environments of their respective dreamers. These alleged realists are finally (and ironically) bound inextricably to the dream for which Nick claims "unaffected scorn" and John claims "fairy tale" status. They are both (as Iowa Bob would have it) "obsessed and *stay* obsessed" (126). The act of re-creating the dreamers' experiences and objectifying their own involvement and insight is the act of the artist seeking order and meaning.

Men in White Dinner Jackets

In another conscious and emphatic evocation of *The Great Gatsby*, Irving develops a recurring image of "the man in the white dinner jacket," a figure whose initial presence is mysterious and ephemeral. In the first chapter of the novel, where the romantic universe of the Arbuthnot-by-the-Sea is once again re-created by the Berry family (as told by John), the ethereal figure first emerges to Mary and Win:

the white sloop sailed toward them. . . . My father caught the mooring line . . . when the man in the white dinner jacket, black slacks, and black dress shoes stepped easily off the deck . . . [he] guided the sloop past the end of the dock. . . . "You're free!" he called to the boat, then. My mother and father claimed they saw no sailors on board, but the sloop slipped away, back to the sea—its yellow lights leaving like sinking glass. . . .
The man's perfect clothes were unaffected by his voyage. For so early in the summer he was very tanned, and he offered my mother and father ciga-rettes from a handsome flat black box. (15)

That this mysterious presence is apparently Arbuthnot, owner of the resort and symbol of success, charm, self-confidence, and Father says, money, establishes an objective correlative in *The Hotel New Hampshire*, at first a symbol of Win Berry's romantic and wholly elu-sive dream.

It is no accident that this figure is later identified by Lilly as the Gatsby figure, for when he first sees his West Egg neighbor at one of his lavish parties, Nick Carraway describes a similarly otherworldly vision: "my eyes fell on Gatsby, standing alone on the marble steps and looking from one group to another with approving eyes. His tanned skin was drawn attractively tight on his face and his short hair looked as though it were trimmed every day" (50). Just as the vision of Gatsby in his "gorgeous pink suit" or white flannels comes to sym-bolize the dream manifested in shallow acquisitiveness, the figure in the white dinner jacket triggers Win Berry to revitalize, or seek once again, the dream of a successful family hotel. Or so we are led to believe by John Berry.

On close examination, however, it becomes clear that while Father is initially inspired by the presence or vision of men in white dinner jackets, they later lose their symbolic power for him, despite the fact that his initial dream continues to remain intact. On the family's return from Vienna, Win *does* fantasize about the Arbuthnot-by-the-Sea; but he explicitly denies imagining the man in the white dinner jacket. Moreover, when the family agrees to buy the ruined resort, he refuses to "see" the owner: "I don't want to see him—if *he* still owns it. . . . I don't want to see the bastard" (409). Lilly, who "saw him all the time—in her sleep" (409), and Franny agree. So the man has, for many members of the family (with the notable exception of John and Lilly), lost his totemic potency.

John, however, requires more direct demystification of the image because he has been the one actually responsible for creating the symbolic connection from the beginning; he has assumed its power over Father and imbued Win with poetic insight which he never really possesses. The night Mother and Father discuss converting the Thompson Female Seminary into the first Hotel New Hampshire, for example, John invents the source of their inspiration: "And I knew that if a white sloop had pulled up to the front porch . . . my mother and father would not have been surprised. If the man in the white dinner jacket, who owned the once exotic Arbuthnot-by-the-Sea, had been there to greet them, they wouldn't have blinked an eye" (67). Furthermore, John deepens the symbolic associations of the image by suggesting the connection between imagination, night, and the man in the white dinner jacket. He assumes Father dreams only "in the darkness, where the imagination is never impeded" (69): "nighttime was the only time the man in the white dinner jacket made an appearance . . . it must have been dark when my father and mother first slept together" (69). "It must have been" is John's speculation, the artist's reconstruction.

Reinforcing his own creative ability to link events and dreams into symbolic constructs, John "entertains" an altogether un-Arbuthnot man in a white dinner jacket on the New Year's Eve Father will begin dreaming of a second Hotel New Hampshire in Vienna: "Of course I knew he was not *the* man in the white dinner jacket; he was lacking the necessary dignity. . . . He was not *our* man in the white dinner

jacket, but he reminded me of him" (186–87). Attempting to hide
this local drunk from Father because he assumes Win's dreams will
be instantly rekindled, John ironically infuses him with romantic
strength: "I hadn't noticed, until I arranged the man in the white
dinner jacket on the couch, how shabby our lobby was . . . the almost elegant man in the white dinner jacket looked—in the Hotel
New Hampshire—like someone from another planet, and I suddenly
didn't want my father to see him" (188).

Father does see him just as he disappears into the night shouting
goodbyes and good luck, but John attributes the mystery to the
figure: "The effect was stunning: the man in the white dinner jacket
stepped out of the light and was gone—as gone as if he were gone to
sea—and my father gaped into the darkness after him" (192) fruit-
lessly calling him back. One could assume Win Berry would be temporarily disappointed and imaginatively titillated by such a gratuitous
event. But it is John, like Nick when he establishes the occasion for
Gatsby to reacquaint himself with Daisy, who literally reinvigorates
the dream: "But I didn't destroy Freud's letter; I gave it to Father,
while the vision of the man in the white dinner jacket was still upon
him" (192). It is now virtually impossible to tell the dancer from the
dance; the vision of the man in the white dinner jacket is upon John.

At this point in John's experience, the vision is unequivocally romantic and positively associated with the idyllic past of the Arbuthnot-by-the-Sea. A dramatic shift of association is, however, about to
occur as John begins to mature into a life that brings pain—the life
of an adult where doom is imminent and sorrow floats.

As they are preparing to leave for Vienna, John has what will become a prophetic "dream that Mother died":

There was the faintest effort of her famous shrug, and the intention of a
shrug in her eyes, which rolled up and out of sight, suddenly, and Father
knew that the man in the white dinner jacket had taken Mother's hand.
    "Okay! No more bears!" Father promised, but Mother was aboard the
white sloop, now, and she went sailing out to sea. (213)

For the very first time, the image of the man in the white dinner
jacket is associated with a dream of death—not Father's dream
(which, of course, indirectly causes Mother's death), but John's: "my
dream of Mother's death was inexact, and I would never dream it
again. Her death—by some considerable stretch of the imagination—

might have been initiated by the man in the white dinner jacket, but no pretty white sloop sailed her away" (231).

John's "considerable stretch of the imagination" and the now ambiguous image of the man in the white dinner jacket is further developed by two references, occurring in ironic juxtaposition, immediately prior to the climactic events at the Viennese hotel. Accompanying him to the marvelous Hotel Sacher where Father indicates to John his sense of personal failure and promises "no more hotels," John sees his father anew—as a man who bears his relative failure with the grace and style of "the richest man in the world, but a man who didn't give a damn." "I wonder where the bartender thought Father was from. From off a yacht, I suppose; from at least the Bristol or the Ambassador or the Imperial. And I realized that Father had never actually needed the white dinner jacket to look the part" (334).

Cognizant (perhaps for the first time) of his Father's unique qualities as a man and a dreamer, John disassociates him from the romantic figure which has now taken on portentous associations soon to be even more ominous. Walking back to their own shabby hotel, John sees a man hurrying past, dressed (inappropriately for the season) in a white dinner jacket. "My father didn't notice the man in the white dinner jacket, but I didn't feel comfortable with this omen, with this reminder; the man in the white dinner jacket, I knew, was dressed for the Opera" (336).

"This omen" completes a symbolic cycle wholly of John's own invention. Entirely oblivious as Father clearly now is, John alone creates the associations with men in white dinner jackets, and in this case, the symbol is unequivocally of impending death—the terrorists are to bomb the Opera sometime during its opening season. And indeed, they are preparing for the act at precisely the moment John sees the man scurrying to the Opera.

But John will reinforce the ambiguity of the Gatsby image at one more critical moment before he meets the "original" man in the white dinner jacket. As the terrorists begin to implement the destructive and anarchistic act for which they have been preparing all along, Father moves into real, as opposed to the dream of, action. Attempting to exert control over the terrorist debacle, he asserts his presence: "Father wanted to know *everything* that was going on. He was a hero; he was on the dock at the old Arbuthnot-by-the-Sea, except *he* was the man in the white dinner jacket—he was in charge" (353).

And how is the active heroism finally represented? Father kills
Ernst, leader of the terrorists, with a Louisville Slugger and is simultaneously blinded as Freud sacrifices his own life to detonate the
bomb car. Heroism and romance form a conflation with death and
pain. The man in the white dinner jacket is suddenly the vehicle of
death as well as of dreams. And so, of course, is Gatsby: "So we drove
on toward death through the cooling twilight" (137).

Much as Gatsby's Daisy, object and symbol of his dream, is ultimately exposed not merely as "careless" but as deadly, so too is Father's dream—as it is manifest in the Viennese hotel—revealed as
apocalyptic nightmare. Moreover, as the nightmare is left behind and
Father returns a rich, though blinded, "hero" inevitably to dream
again, the ubiquitous man in the white dinner jacket once more sur-
faces. But Father has long since divested himself of any romantic attachment or symbolic awareness of the image; he simply refuses to
"see" old Arbuthnot, even when the sale of the resort depends on an
exchange between someone in the family and the original man in the
white dinner jacket.

It is fitting indeed that Frank, family "agent," and John visit him.
For however much he has transmogrified the youthful, benign, and
ephemeral image into the far more "realistic" and paradoxical symbol
of death in the dream, John remains attached—like Nick Carraway
does—to the romantic vision. The man in the white dinner jacket—
urbane, gorgeously tanned, and elegant smoker of long cigarettes
from a smooth black box—is an old man dying, appropriately, of em-
physema: "An almost sky-blue mole was sprouting on old Arbuthnot's face and both his ears were painted a vivid purple with a gentian
violet, an old-fashioned fungicide. It was as if a giant fungus were
consuming Arbuthnot from the inside out" (413).

Romantic figure transformed into horror movie monster. The almost allegorical reversal of the romantic image of Arbuthnot to this
grotesquely distorted being is further deepened by the character that
is exposed. Vicious anti-Semite that he is, Arbuthnot wants to meet
the Berry sons in order to ensure that no Jews will own his ruined
resort. Moreover, he remembers Freud as "a dumb Jewish animal
trainer" who "tried to train a bear, but the bear ate him!" (412). In
Father's original story, Arbuthnot was sympathetic toward Freud and
made at worst a cryptic remark about the then imminent fate of the
Jews in Europe: "It's a good thing he got out of Europe when he did,
you know. Europe's going to be no place for Jews" (16).

So while Fitzgerald's Gatsby retains throughout his life the qualities of innocence that allow him, among other things, to fraternize with Jewish gangsters in the anti-Semitic world of East and West Egg Long Island, Arbuthnot's unmasking reveals no such innocence. On the contrary, in Irving's world, the gorgeous suntanned skin is transformed into the unnatural violet of a chemically treated face, the elegant cigarette box foreshadows an emphysemiac's coffin, and an earlier, apparently sympathetic attitude toward Jews is revealed as an obsessive hatred which consumes Arbuthnot from the inside out.

Unlike Arbuthnot, however, Father retains an innocence absolutely comparable to Gatsby's, though he is shielded from the consequences of that innocence by a loving family. For John, on the other hand, the demystification of Arbuthnot—of all symbols of illusory dreams—is a necessary prelude to his own maturation as a man and as an incipient artist. Despite the fact that he is now able and willing to devote himself to preserving his father's innocence by becoming the caretaker of his illusions, he does so with the complete self-consciousness of the artist who perceives the grim realities of life but simultaneously chooses to nourish benign—if not transcendent—dreams. And like Nick who also returns to the familiar world of the conservative, and very American, midwest (where he is "part of that"), John returns to the unspoiled New England coast, an ersatz hotel, and a family to whom he has contributed new members and new life.

"Life Is Serious But Art Is Fun!"

The King of the Mice is first introduced to the Berry family by Freud in a cable to them describing the Viennese hotel to which they will soon be committed:

THERE WAS A STREET CLOWN CALLED KING OF THE MICE: HE TRAINED RODENTS, HE DID HOROSCOPES, HE COULD IMPERSONATE NAPOLEON, HE COULD MAKE DOGS FART ON COMMAND. ONE NIGHT HE JUMPED OUT HIS WINDOW WITH ALL HIS PETS IN A BOX. WRITTEN ON THE BOX WAS THIS: "LIFE IS SERIOUS BUT ART IS FUN!" I HEAR HIS FUNERAL WAS A PARTY. A STREET ARTIST HAD KILLED HIMSELF. . . . IT IS HARD WORK AND GREAT ART TO MAKE LIFE NOT SO SERIOUS. (205)

The story of the King of the Mice and the exhortation to avoid his end, "Keep passing the open windows," are among the most important of several leitmotifs in *The Hotel New Hampshire*, leitmotifs that Irving describes as "little litanies, little choruses in a simple hymn."[12]

That both Lilly and Fehlgeburt fail to keep passing open windows is particularly ironic because, like the King of the Mice, they too die for art—or, more accurately, they each commit suicide because neither believes she can change, escape, or transcend the seriousness of life or transform it through art. And once again, *The Great Gatsby* serves to typify great art that is both uniquely American and, for Irving, seems to have the potential to "make life not so serious."

"You know," Fehlgeburt would tell me, "the single ingredient in American literature that distinguishes it from other literatures of the world is a kind of giddy, illogical hopefulness. It is quite technically sophisticated while remaining ideologically naïve." (309)

Trapped in what she accepts as the ideologically sophisticated rhetoric and logic of the Austrian anarchists, Fehlgeburt's passion for art, and specifically her love affair with the American novel, creates an irreconcilable tension which makes it increasingly painful for her to define her life in other than psychologically schizophrenic terms:

"That passage. That lovely passage, that *ending*—to *The Great Gatsby*— . . . I don't know, but—somehow—it makes me want to go to the United States. I mean, it's against my politics—your country—I know that. But that *ending*, all of it—somehow—is just so *beautiful*. It makes me want to *be* there. I mean, there's no *sense* to it, but I would just like to be in the United States." (261)

John, himself a student of American literature, is drawn to Fehlgeburt precisely because she is a caring person whose political associations belie her artistic and essentially moral nature. Furthermore, he associates these qualities directly with the object of her study and affections: "Her weakness—among the radicals—was her fondness for literature, especially for the romance that is American literature. . . . It was the romantic part of her that wasn't quite dead. . . ." (262). Even Ernst recognizes the nature of Fehlgeburt's character and attributes her suicide to the moral compunction of a romantic: " 'Fehlgeburt had a fatal case of romanticism,' Ernst said. 'She always questioned the *means*' " (346).

Like Fehlgeburt, Lilly too is moved to passionate grief by both the

aesthetic beauty of *The Great Gatsby* and by her realization that her
father is a Gatsby-like figure in search of an impossible dream. Unlike
Fehlgeburt's, however, Lilly's despair is not ultimately related to a
moral and spiritual schism between her life and art; Lilly's inability
to keep passing the open windows is aesthetic and existential despair,
the failure of the artist:

> There's no point in writing a book if you don't *think* it can be as good as
> *The Great Gatsby*. I mean, it's all right if you fail—if the finished book just
> isn't, somehow, very good—but you have to believe it *can* be very good be-
> fore you start. And sometimes that damn ending to *The Great Gatsby* just
> wipes me out before I can get started. (376)

Indeed, Lilly can neither execute a novel comparable in beauty and
style to *Gatsby*, nor can she maintain the paradox of dream and reality
in creative tension. Her last novel, *Evening of the Mind* (which John
says should have been titled *Certain Failure*) "was about the death of
dreams, it was about how hard the dreams die" (420). Lilly commits
suicide because, as she quotes Donald Justice, "I do not think the
ending can be right." For Lilly "illogical hopefulness" is impossible;
she is the King of the Mice, for whom "it is hard work and great art
to make life not so serious."

"Rich Passion . . . for Extremes"

The fabric of *The Hotel New Hampshire* is woven of many threads,
not the least of which represents a commentary on the nature of
American literature. At the same time Irving embeds that commentary in the action and nature of his characters, he attempts, through
John Berry, to emulate—and simultaneously reinvigorate—the classic
American romance. Having experimented with earlier (and traditionally more British than American) literary prototypes and modes in
Garp, he moves in *Hotel* to the genre and tradition with which he is
finally more culturally familiar and in which he is more imaginatively
secure. And however much he eschews academic criticism and belit-
tles the arch, and often absurd, contortions of the academy in its critical pursuits, Irving is a formally trained, broadly read student of
literature, just as his narrator is. It is therefore not surprising that he
has a kind of double vision which embodies human experience in a

symbolic construct at the same time it reflects on the nature and tradition of that construct.

In *The Hotel New Hampshire*, Irving sets out to write, perhaps quite consciously, an American romance with contemporary twists. Yet in many ways, the novel itself seems to beg the question. While he moves freely on his canvas—often defying realistic character development, inventing bizarre scenes, rejecting conventional mores, as romancers traditionally do—Irving nevertheless involves us in unassimilated social issues that most genuine romance ultimately supersedes or transcends. The horror of rape, for example, while providing evidence of Irving's deep human concern (and earlier treated brilliantly in *Garp*), is presented here primarily as a social and cultural issue; it is *discussed* more often than dramatically embodied in affective human experiences.

Likewise, other "socially relevant" themes (e.g., racism, feminism, anti-Semitism, terrorism) frequently intrude so forcefully into the otherwise fantastic world of the novel that they become preeminent and, at least temporarily, confuse or obfuscate the tones and rhythms of romance. Irving himself reinforced the difficulty of reconciling the elements of romance with those of social consciousness when he described (inaccurately, we think) Franny as the protagonist and hero of *Hotel*.[13] While she no doubt is a strong and admirable female character, Win and John Berry and their pursuit of the American dream represent the novel's most significant emotional and imaginative foci. Indeed, when Irving does try to integrate the socially relevant themes he explores with the romance mode—as he does in the absurd punishment of Franny's rapist, Chipper Dove—he fails both as artist and as concerned humanist: the result in this scene (and in several others) is a simultaneous trivialization of romance *and* polemic.

It is perhaps true that such failures in *Hotel* can be attributed to the artistic dissonance these contrary interests, modes, and styles reflect. For it is nevertheless the case, as Hawthorne so forcefully made it, that the American artist is striving to create "a neutral territory, somewhere between the real world and fairy-land, where the Actual and the Imaginary may meet, and each imbue itself with the nature of the other."[14] Lilly's inability to create that "neutral territory" is sharply contrasted to John Berry's ability to do precisely that: "to discover," as Chase puts it, "a putative unity in disunity or to rest at last among irreconcilables."[15] And Irving portrays John's success in a manner that is meant to represent his own aspirations as writer of American romance, "the profound poetry of disorder."[16]

The Hotel New Hampshire suffers from unnecessary length, some silliness that is meant to be more like "the stirring instabilities of American humor"[17] found in *Garp* and inherited from Twain and Faulkner, and from an uneasy inability to imbue sufficiently this fantasy world with profundity whose weight it simply cannot bear. It is, nevertheless, an interesting experiment, an experiment that attempts to bring both continuity and a new voice to the literary tradition it honors and imitates. As Chase argues, "the fact seems to be that the history of the American novel is not only the history of the rise of realism but also of the repeated rediscovery of the uses of romance, and that this will continue to be so."[18]

Irving's most recent novel, *The Cider House Rules*, would seem to reinforce Chase's thesis.

Chapter Seven
The Cider House Rules:
Novel as Polemic

In the spring of 1985 William Morrow, Irving's new publisher, brought out *The Cider House Rules*, his sixth novel to be published in seventeen years. Like *Garp* and *The Hotel New Hampshire* it is a large work—again Dickensian in scope—and like those two novels the book continues his emphasis on narrative rather than on style or subtlety of theme. This book confirms the permanence of Irving's shift, first obvious in *Garp*, from the "academic" novel to the novel of mass appeal; as in his previous two books, Irving here reaffirms fiction that is fully "accessible" and "entertaining" as opposed to that which is elusive and self-reflexive.[1]

Missing from the new book, however, are bears, Austria, wrestling, and motorcycles (things he now calls "security blankets"[2]) and present is a pronounced thematic militancy. "I honestly believe that this book is very different from anything I've ever written," Irving has claimed. "It is a book with a polemic."[3] So it is, and *Cider House* will, therefore, extend and intensify the controversy surrounding Irving's fiction.

"Waiting and Seeing"

The eleven chapters of *Cider House* move the novel's straightforward plot from the last two decades of the nineteenth century through roughly the first two-thirds of the twentieth. They tell the linked stories of Dr. Wilbur Larch and the orphan Homer Wells.

At St. Cloud's, Maine, a minimal outpost of New England civilization (the name has climatological, not ostensibly religious significance), the young working-class physician, educated in the miseries of the poor and the inequities of the abortion laws by an internship at the Boston Lying-In Hospital, founds an orphanage and a clandestine abortion clinic. Except for a World War I tour of duty in France, Dr.

Larch lives and serves at St. Cloud's for the remainder of his very long life. At Boston Lying-In he had observed a heartless and senseless refusal to face the tragedies of unwanted pregnancy; at a primitive and illegal "clinic" (called enigmatically "Off Harrison") he had witnessed the inevitable results. Aware that there was no viable role for him in Boston, he had joined the Maine State Board of Medical Examiners. Whatever else might happen, Larch realized that "he was an obstetrician; he delivered babies into the world. His colleagues called this 'the Lord's work.' And he was an abortionist; he delivered mothers, too. His colleagues called this 'the Devil's work,' but it was *all* the Lord's work to Wilbur Larch" (75). Where a choice was medically feasible, the decision would always be the woman's.

Larch is assisted in this sad if necessary labor by two celibate and selfless women, nurses Edna and Angela. As the years of unending effort and spartan existence stretch on, the doctor (having tried sex and rejected it) finds solace only in working for his orphans and in a modest drug addiction; he occasionally sniffs ether.

In spite of his self-denial, Dr. Larch is granted the love and respect of one special orphan, Homer Wells, who (through no fault of his own) has been unsuccessfully adopted several times and remains "the boy who belonged to St. Cloud's" (15). Homer will become, everyone believes, the doctor's protegé and eventual successor. While still a child and with no formal education, under Larch's tutelage he gradually assumes the role of a medical intern specializing in obstetrics and—inevitably, given St. Cloud's mission—abortion. But when Homer is only thirteen years old he finds a fetus on the ground near the hospital's incinerator, and the result of his ensuing attempt to understand the nature of emerging life will be the rejection of abortion—not in theory, nor for Dr. Larch, but unquestionably for himself. Though a skilled midwife before he is twenty and an able assistant at numerous abortions, Homer Wells would conclude that whatever the justifications "and whatever you call what you do," aborting a living fetus is "killing it" (169).

Homer's existence is enlivened chiefly by evening readings of Dickens and Brontë and, especially as he reaches puberty, by his relationship with Melony, the oldest female orphan at St. Cloud's and a psychological and physical bully. If Larch instructs Homer in "the products of conception," Melony teaches him all about the process itself. This troubled relationship ends when a golden couple arrives for an abortion. After it is concluded, the young man, Wally Worthington, son of a wealthy apple farmer on Maine's healthy sea coast, and the young woman, Candy Kendall, lovely daughter of a lobsterman, invite the bedazzled Homer to return with them to the Maine of sun and sea; Homer, at a saddened Larch's urging, willingly goes. In so doing he breaks a promise never to leave Melony, and sets in motion her long search for him.

Homer has been pulled away from St. Cloud's by the powerful attractions of instant love and friendship, but he has also been pushed by his growing conflict with Dr. Larch over the practice of abortion. Larch wants not only Homer's approval; he wishes the young man to commit himself to the orphanage and the work of his illegal clinic. For all his dedication to the orphanage and his love for Dr. Larch, however, Homer dreams of a family life where everything is *wanted*. The Worthington apple orchards in Heart's Rock and the Kendall lobster dock at Heart's Haven provide such an existence. With appropriate Hawthornesque symbolism, Irving transports Homer from the continually overcast and gloomy inland valley of St. Cloud's where even the cigar smoke and sawdust of long departed loggers still hang in the air (there literal and figurative darkness broods over all) to Ocean View, a farm blessed with sunlight and moving air.

Homer's intended visit becomes a permanent residence as the senior Worthingtons accept him into the family and the business. But two clear dilemmas remain to trouble Homer's pastoral escape. In the first place, his loyalty to Dr. Larch remains, along with a latent sense of responsibility to the work of the orphanage—*all* the work of the orphanage. Second, Homer's immediate and deepening love for Candy is a constant agony to him and when the second world war allows the adventurous Wally to enter flight training, her early affection for Homer turns into an abiding love.

When Wally's B-24 bomber is lost over Burma, Homer and Candy, having convinced themselves that the Wally they both love is dead, conceive a child that neither wishes to destroy. Pleading an obligation to lend St. Cloud's some well-deserved support, the couple moves to the orphanage where (unbeknownst to Wally's mother and Candy's father) she gives birth to a healthy son whom they name Angel. During a long and very happy Maine winter they enjoy "the life of a young married couple" (399) and Homer—still rejecting any role in abortions—learns more about pediatrics.

Then word comes that Wally is indeed alive, though paralyzed from the waist down, and being sent home. The couple returns to the

ry he reads, since any story is "newly informed by the recent expe-
nces in life" (113) and the story, in turn, helps shape the reader's
n existence. The narrator of *Cider House* knows that "sometimes the
erest in the literature isn't in the literature—the boys' division was
audience like any other: self-interest, personal memories, their se-
t anxieties crept into their perceptions of what they heard (regard-
s of what Charles Dickens had done. . . .)" (215). The critic is
ays in danger of failing to recognize just how oblique, if useful,
h perceptions may be, or just how obscure is the point at which
and fiction really intersect.

Hence for fiction to "work," in Irving's view, for it to have an im-
t that is not defined solely in aesthetic or conceptual terms by the
ached intellect, both the novelist and the reader must do that now
haracteristic and risky thing—identify with, "admire and care
" the characters.[10] Irony, an especially modern form of self-de-
se, must be abandoned or at least contained, the distance between
racter and reader be reduced, the illusion of imaginative reality
braced rather than repudiated, and the conviction of literature's
nan value reaffirmed. Above all, the writer must develop—and the
er share—his personal vision in order to create a fiction that is
al in the existential, if not Dickensian, sense. As Jane Hill has
, Irving "prefers to define moral fiction as fiction that adheres to
individual writer's vision of truth."[11]

"Polemic"

ider House Rules does possess a vigorous personal vision. It also of-
a richly textured group of characters focused on Dr. Larch at St.
d's and on Homer Wells and Candy at Heart's Rock and Heart's
en. The reader is indeed absorbed into their purely human drama
for the most part, they do earn our admiration. But the Dicken-
literature of accessibility to which Irving aspires brings with it
in difficulties.

y the end of the novel Homer abandons distinctions in aesthetic
h between Dickens and Brontë, because "both [authors] gave
huge entertainment and instruction" (550). Homer's terms here
lightly altered versions of Irving's own: "Art and entertainment
t contradictions," he has argued.[12] In theory the reader may
. That there may be contradictions when these goals are con-

coast, their idyll over. Homer claims to have adopted the baby
("we've kind of adopted a baby together," Candy tells her father
[416]) and when Wally returns, Candy—who both loves and feels a
great loyalty to Wally—confirms the fiction by marrying her childhood sweetheart. When the pain and anxiety of these divided loves
had first become apparent, Homer had demanded that Candy choose
between them. She could, however, only promise to "wait and see"
(347), a refrain that is repeated throughout the remainder of the
novel. Later Homer complains that all life holds for him is "waiting
and seeing" (359); for the next fifteen years they all wait and see—
accepting an understandable but dishonest and increasingly strained
status quo.

Dr. Larch, however, refuses to wait and see; he has never abandoned hope that Homer will one day replace him. To that end he
creates an elaborate fraud; writing the history of the orphanage and
detailed reports on the subsequent lives of the adopted children for an
ever more intrusive board of trustees, Larch establishes and docu-
ments the identity of a well-trained prolife pediatrician, using the
name of a former orphan who had actually died at St. Cloud's. Faking
college and medical school records and a history of missionary service
in the Third World, Larch prepares for the day when he can convince
Homer—superbly trained but formally uneducated—that he must return and can safely do so by assuming that identity.

This goal is in fact finally achieved when a complicated series of
events at Ocean View at last forces Homer to acknowledge Angel's
parentage. The farm's migratory apple pickers, blacks from the
South, arrive for the harvest under their straw boss, Mr. Rose, a
quick man with a knife. Accompanying him this year are his teenage
daughter Rose and her baby. Angel, just entering young manhood,
is smitten with love for her and, in his vigorous pursuit of the young
woman, he discovers that she is once again pregnant, this time by her
own father. In the ensuing turmoil Rose stabs her father and disappears with her child; before she leaves, however, Homer aborts the
incestuously conceived fetus.

The necessity of performing that operation, the self-admission
brought on by Mr. Rose that Homer, too, has broken rules much like
those intended to govern workers living in the cider house, the conse-
quent need to confess to Wally and Angel and, finally, the accidental
death of Dr. Larch caused by his ether addiction—all conspire to end
Homer's long evasion of his true destiny.

Earlier, when her tenacious search for Homer culminated in a sudden appearance at Ocean View, Melony had instantly recognized Angel's parentage. Amidst an irregular and often violent life, and despite her ambivalent feelings for Homer resulting from his broken promise, Melony had always clung to a vision of Homer as a potential hero: "I somehow thought you'd end up doin' somethin' better than ballin' a poor cripple's wife and pretendin' your own child ain't your own," she tells Homer (469). "I always thought you'd end up like the old man" (470). Homer himself had, as a child, often meditated on the opening lines of *David Copperfield*: "whether I shall turn out to be the hero of my own life, or whether that station will be held by anybody else, these pages must show" (79). Homer's final return to St. Cloud's as the fictitious Dr. F. Stone, whose impeccable reputation and well-known abhorrence at the thought of abortion will allow him to carry on Dr. Larch's lifetime commitment to the delivery of mothers as well as babies, would now allow him to answer that question affirmatively. The long bildungsroman is over.

St. Larch and David Copperfield

"Especially now, after *Garp*," Irving said in an interview, "I'm very conscious of attempting to make my narrative as absolutely linear as possible." By 1982 he had come to lament the "convoluted flow" of his first four books and suggested that his work then in progress—*The Hotel New Hampshire*—would consequently be more direct and straightforward.[4] Although at least one early reviewer has called *Cider House* a "slog," largely blaming a rambling and "ramshackle" plot,[5] his latest work, even more clearly than *Hotel New Hampshire*, reflects Irving's new intentions. Comparison with *Water-Method Man* or *Garp*, for instance, emphasizes the clear, uncomplicated line of plot development that Irving now prefers. Except for the appropriate retrospective views necessitated by the emergence of new characters, Irving's only major exception is his return, early in the book, to Dr. Larch's initial history and route to St. Cloud's; otherwise his story is told from birth to death. Homer, who also emerges in the novel's first chapter, is developed continuously from infancy through middle age.

As numerous references in the novel, its novelistic devices, and Irving's comments make clear, the author's deep respect for Dickens (and nineteenth-century fiction in general) strongly influences this decision. However, such fiction has traditionally emphasized not only

plot but character, already a major fictional element i by the time of *The Water-Method Man*. His method h he claims, to start with deeply imagined characters an for the actions that seem appropriate to them.[6] Since I into the writing of *Cider House* "before abortion ev story," and only then because of the logic inherent i orphanage director, the claim would appear to have r first three novels, moreover, he had come to feel th creating characters that he "didn't like" and that he r to write about people whom he "absolutely did not *ac* prisingly, therefore, Dr. Larch (whose nickname is Homer Wells (who eventually assumes this secular sa roes in the sense that Garp and Win Berry are; the domestic drama in which Hannes Graff, Bogus T nameless narrator of *The 158-Pound Marriage* (all esse so familiar to modern fiction) could never exist. Inde characters in *Cider House* whom Irving does not seem mire; characterization is marked by a kind of Di which embraces even the would-be villains.

Nurse Caroline, a minor character who is "tou clearly admired by Irving, finds Dickens a "sentime but the "superiority of the nineteenth-century nov where implied in *Cider House*. Nor is Irving's enthu ter of popular fiction merely conjured up in sup novel; in his 1979 article, "In Defense of Sentin knowledges his unqualified respect for Dickens, willing to risk the sentimental because "his kindne his belief in our dignity" demanded that he confron of his characters.[9] Though Dr. Larch, an austere an physican, never succumbs to Dickens's appeal (I *Anatomy* and *The New England Journal of Medicine*) Melony personally develop in relation to and with reading Dickens and Charlotte Brontë. For Melo define the nature of spiritual independence and pain; for Homer, *Great Expectations* and *David C* rereads, often aloud, during the entire novel) wo explore the orphan's situation and sensibility—he tion.

Irving implies, therefore, that the value of suc nurturing reciprocity that exists between the r

sciously linked, as they often seem to be in popular fiction, is also true. When the instruction is intended to entertain or—as may be partially the case with *Cider House Rules*—when the entertainment is intended to instruct, the novelist may experience distracting temptations. Irving's comments on the novel immediately following its publication are especially interesting in this regard: "I didn't set out to write a novel about quote-unquote abortion. And I certainly didn't expect that the so-called controversy over abortion would become such an issue. But if this book can contribute anything to what I consider the correct political vision on that issue, all the better." There is, it should be noted, something ominous about the phrase "correct political vision," especially in light of another earlier quoted remark on the same occasion: "I honestly believe that this book is very different from anything I've ever written. It is a book with a polemic."[13] From an aesthetic perspective, there is nothing particularly comforting about these comments.

In the past Irving has vigorously and repeatedly rejected not only autobiographical fiction but "sociology" as well: "I'm not a sociological writer, nor should I be considered a social realist in any way." He has argued that the impulse to "reduce literature to sociology, history, or psychology" is "a sick instinct."[14] Yet, in addition to describing *Cider House* as a "polemic," he has several times referred to it as an "historical novel," apparently alluding to the modern history of abortion in America: "I wanted it to seem like something that really happened, not like something I invented."[15] (This impression is strengthened by the novel's eight pages of notes, most of which document various medical realities and past practices relating to abortion.) Therefore, it is not so much the Dickens of *Great Expectations* whom we are reminded of in *Cider House* as it is the Dickens of *Hard Times*: a writer with a clear social thesis regarding an historical reality.

When Irving began, he has several times said, he had only wanted to write an orphan novel (hinting to one interviewer about certain surprisingly autobiographical connections with the subject[16]); the logic of abortion only occurred to him later. But the development of the novel along these lines has not lessened the significance of the abortion theme for him or for the reader. If the character and activity of Dr. Larch had ultimately to be determined by situational logic— "what doctor would be most sympathetic to performing abortions but the doctor who delivered unwanted babies, then cared for them in an orphanage?"[17]—the subject cannot help becoming central to the novel's basic concerns, regardless of Irving's protest against what one admiring reviewer has termed the valuable "public dimension" of the book.[18]

"Choice"

Though the issue of abortion is supposedly unresolved in the novel (Irving claims personally to recognize almost every approach to the controversy[19]) and though the plot is built around Dr. Larch's commitment to it as an act of "deliverance" and Homer's early repudiation of it as "murder," there is never any doubt where Irving stands. This is an outspoken, "pro-choice" polemic. We must acknowledge and understand—even approve—Homer's refusal of Larch's mission, but the novel's weight is always behind the doctor. Nor is this a qualified endorsement; in every instance Larch affirms the woman's "choice" (the word reverberates through the novel) regardless of her situation—his only reservations are medical. When the affluent Candy and Wally arrive at St. Cloud's for an abortion it is merely for "practical" reasons; already in love and perfectly capable of telling their parents the truth, "they were simply stunned at the prospect of having to derail their perfect plans—of *having* to get married ahead of schedule" (150). Earlier in the novel we witness truly painful pregnancies: girls raped by fathers, women whose grinding poverty precludes the luxury of birth. But Candy's almost irrelevant and certainly trivial motive makes the issue perfectly clear; the question must never be the justification behind the choice but the choice itself.

However caught up in the author's generosity of plot and character, then, the reader of *Cider House* is returned again and again to the basic dilemma: whose right—mother's or child's—must be recognized? Though at times Dr. Larch's arguments become tired clichés or angry harangues, there are also moments of simple eloquence: "he would deliver babies. He would deliver mothers, too" (75). And it may be, as Benjamin DeMott has argued, that we owe Irving a debt of gratitude for his willingness to probe sympathetically this ever more controversial and painful issue.[20] Yet as "polemic" the novel is seriously flawed and since Irving's "correct political vision" sometimes distorts the book's larger theme—the problematical nature of personal and social "rules"—the difficulties with Irving's new fiction are considerable.

Fish, Fetus, Soul

Early in the novel Homer finds a dead fetus accidentally dropped near the hospital incinerator; and, since Dr. Larch is not only his spiritual father but also responsible for the presence of that fetus, the ensuing dialogue is critical. Larch tries to explain a pregnant woman's choice to Homer. If the child is unwanted and she "simply can't make herself stop" (81) the pregnancy, she may come to St. Cloud's to deliver an orphan. But if she refuses to have the child she may also come to St. Cloud's—to be delivered. "So she kills it," (81) Homer says with the abrupt candor and directness of a child. "I stop it," Larch replies.

> "Tell me again, what's *stopping* it called?" asked Homer Wells.
> "An abortion," Dr. Larch said. (81)

And Larch persists in the language of avoidance: "abortion," "aborted fetus," "embryo." But eventually not only his terminology but also his basic argument—"In a way, Homer, it was never alive" (80)—ceases to satisfy Homer:

> . . . Larch knew what he was doing—and for whom. But that quick and not-quick stuff: it didn't work for Homer Wells. You can *call* it a fetus, or an embryo, or the products of conception, thought Homer Wells, but whatever you call it, it's alive. And whatever you do to it, Homer thought—and whatever you call what you do—you're killing it. . . . Let Larch call it whatever he wants, thought Homer Wells. It's his choice—if it's a fetus, to him, that's fine. It's a baby to me, thought Homer Wells. If Larch has a choice, I have a choice, too. (169)

Homer realizes that Larch's original verbal evasion represents not intellectual or moral failure but an intended kindness and a clear point of view: Larch knows what he is doing. But, in this passage, so does the adolescent Homer. He will eventually accept Larch's argument that abortion is necessary and that the obstetrician actually has *no* choice (whether or not he finds a way to deny the life of the fetus) but Irving's polemic never really moves us beyond the basic conflict indicated in Homer's speech.

Inherent in the Larch-Homer controversy, of course, are two opposing views of life implied but never openly examined—the secular and the religious. Larch, who "didn't think anyone had a soul," (57) and who seems to jest ironically at the cosmos in his nightly prayers, clearly and repeatedly implies a definition that equates life with a postnatal *identity*: "I don't even remember *you* when you were born," he tells Homer; "you didn't *become* you until later" (101). Homer's decision to call the fetus a "baby" and to recognize it as "alive" is consistent with his conclusion that "the fetus has a soul" (513). Homer's unexplained religious view surprises the reader (where did he acquire it?) and outrages Larch: "he believes that a creature that lives like a fish has a soul?" (514) Larch cries out in frustration.

Never fully articulated or even, perhaps, realized, this vital conflict settles into stalemate early in the novel and simply lingers—acting as a brake on the plot which it helps set in motion and distracting the reader from the theme of which it is a part—until near the end when it suddenly dissipates. The issue is not whether we can expect Irving to resolve so fundamental a division between ways of seeing the problem, but rather the question of his willingness to raise the subject without dramatizing its complexity. The intelligent and dedicated Dr. Larch, whose life has been focused narrowly on abortion for years, could well be expected to hold more subtle views than he does. Marked from his childhood by a similar thoughtful integrity, Homer should be able to get beneath the contradictions in his own position; both men appear too easily satisfied. Beyond Homer's, Irving raises no credible arguments for the theological view; its advocates are smug and legalistic doctors and simple social conformists. Since Larch implies but never really articulates the position that "life" begins only with perceptual independence and hence with personal identity—with consciousness—those readers who accept Homer's essentially theological definition must feel betrayed when, after a long hold-out, he abandons that perspective and dedicates his life to what is, for them, "the Devil's work": "After the first one, thought Homer Wells, this might get easier. Because he knew now that he couldn't play God in the worst sense; if he could operate on Rose Rose, how could he refuse to help a stranger? How could he refuse anyone? Only a god makes that kind of decision. I'll just give them what they want, he thought. An orphan or an abortion" (535). There is, of course, a logic to Homer's decision. But when the narrator observes, as Homer begins the abortion of Rose's child, that "he did not divert his eye from witnessing the miracle," even a confirmed pro-choice advocate may find his use of words curious. For these words to embody the significance Irving seems to intend, much that is missing in the novel would have to be supplied.

House Rules

Irving's "polemic," then, is weak not so much because it fails to resolve the dilemma, or because it takes sides, but because it fails to explore adequately the rich, if painful, ambiguities of the issue. Rather than a sufficiently meaningful dramatization of the complexities, it offers us a showy kind of concern for the subject itself. Critics like Benjamin DeMott who, in his gratitude for the author's serious treatment of a most important subject, find *Cider House* "Irving's first truly valuable book," transfer their approval from *treatment* to *topic*. DeMott, like Irving himself, recognizes that ours is "an age ill at ease with the notion that art can have a subject," or more precisely, an age that suspects that no subjects exist "except language, the death of feeling or the artist's proud (or nervous) separation from society."[21] We have attempted to show that in *Garp* Irving brilliantly demonstrates such subjects *do* exist, but that it is their treatment that determines their value—both humanistically and aesthetically.

Beyond the polemical failure—to enlarge significantly our sympathy and tolerance—the treatment of the abortion topic obscures, even retards, development of the more inclusive themes of *Cider House Rules*. The larger significance of "choice" involves the tension between freedom and restraint in a whole range of human situations, and Irving would appear to have set out to examine the "rules" that result from that tension, the abortion law being only one. It is in the nature of things that these rules are both valuable and destructive, essential to public and personal life and necessary to repudiate.

The rules of the book's title are, of course, literally those regulations posted in the apple pickers' dormitory of the Ocean View Orchard's cider house, rules intended to order the behavior of men and women whose transient lives would appear to offer the perfect model for lawlessness. The pickers, usually Southern blacks, are seen as aliens and are therefore thought to need the rules that Maine farmers assume they would not naturally possess. A community (fruit farm or nation) may be judged by the rules it imposes and Olive Worthington's rules are essentially benign; six of the nine posted are designed to insure the workers' own safety. These rules, always ignored, are eventually discovered to be irrelevant, however; as Mr. Rose, the pickers' straw boss, makes clear to Homer, every group has its own rules. Sometimes these separate sets of rules complement each other; frequently they are at odds.

That Irving intends the cider house rules to provide not only the book's title but also its major metaphor, becomes clear as one moves into the novel. Rules governing abortion must sometimes be broken, Larch concludes; other values alter and qualify society's attempt to discipline itself. Society must contend with love, the power of sexual desire, the inequities of its economic and social system, even with its own customs. (Homer "learned the real purpose of the drive-in" was "to tease oneself and one's date into a state of sexual frenzy" [254].) On the other hand, Homer's examination of dead fetuses alerts him to their humanness, their life—hence their rights. The nature of rules is complex.

In addition to abortion, the novel abounds in other situations where such tensions exist. Several chapter titles allude directly to this dilemma. Chapter five, "Homer Breaks a Promise," refers to his flight from St. Cloud's after having promised Melony never to abandon her. On one hand, that promise surely binds him; on the other, it is made under duress and at a specific time in his development. When he breaks that promise other forces are at work in his life, primarily newly found love, friendship, and the desire to go where life is "wanted." Chapter eight is called "Opportunity Knocks" and though that is Wally's name for his B-24, it better describes the position of Candy and Homer, whose inescapable attraction to each other strengthens as the distance between Maine and Burma weakens their responsibilities to Wally. Chapter ten—"Fifteen Years"—measures the period of compromise during which Candy, Homer, and Wally try to live within the conflicting rules of love, loyalty, marriage, and desire.

The novel's final chapter focuses the metaphor; in "Breaking the Rules" several aspects of the theme come together. The unavoidable yet rules-breaking love of Homer and Candy had earlier produced a child, Angel, whose adolescent love for Mr. Rose's daughter emphasizes the rules different races make for themselves and for each other. Rose seems capable of reciprocating Angel's love, but she is pregnant by her own father; the tension is thus complicated: personal, sexual, familial.

Earlier Mr. Rose had explained to Homer that the blacks had their own cider house rules. Now, as Homer attempts to intercede on behalf of Angel and Rose (he is worried "about someone being hurt. . . . About the rules" [519]), Mr. Rose quietly hands Homer the stub of a candle left behind by Homer and Candy when they had made guilty love in the cider house: "that 'gainst the rules, ain't it?" (519) he knowingly asks Homer.

In *Cider House*, then, Irving explores many aspects of a paradox created by the conflict between rules and human realities, between social law and personal freedom, between abstract value and biological life. Homer, who as an orphan without a past is naturally a moral explorer, must finally discover at least a tentative resolution of the paradoxes surrounding not only his own life but that of abortion as well—though the form that resolution takes may not fully convince the reader. He will perform abortions, surrender Candy to Wally, and move back to St. Cloud's, all in opposition to his desire, though not against his will. The rules of society and those we establish for ourselves are at best uneasy compromises between contending absolutes. Yet society and the individual must finally live by such compromises, Irving seems to suggest, though they are flimsy and temporary structures at best. (It is interesting to note that even Melony, the novel's outlaw, gradually accommodates herself to the world around her.)

That this vital and universal theme remains only partially developed in the novel, more potential than actual, can in part be attributed to Irving's polemic, to his tendency to adopt the instruction, as well as the entertainment, of nineteenth-century fiction.

More Artists

Angel, whom "Rose had introduced to love and to imagination [the thematic focus of *Garp*], would one day be a novelist," (550) we are told at the book's end. "To Candy, a novelist was also what Homer Wells had become—for a novelist, in Candy's opinion, was also a kind of impostor doctor, but a good doctor nonetheless" (550). Novelists find patients "they can't cure," Irving has recently said, and "tell their stories instead."[22] These comments remind us of the line late in *Garp*: "A novelist is a doctor who sees only terminal cases" (570).

Artist figures abound in Irving's novels and, in *Cider House*, it is not Homer, but Larch, of course, who holds that position. Not only is he the historian of St. Cloud's (a metaphor for art Irving has often employed), but he creates and destroys in ways appropriate only to God, or to the artist.

As historian, Larch interprets as much as records the world around him. His first experience with the creative restructuring of existence occurs when he invents a mild heart condition for Homer and writes it into the orphan's records so that he will not be drafted into the impending war. When forces from outside St. Cloud's (in the form of a meddling board of orphanage trustees) threaten his abortion clinic, Larch's imaginative re-creation of reality becomes more extensive. He gives new life to a long dead orphan named Fuzzy Stone (and eventually "kills off" Homer by a more serious heart disease) by means of a series of fictitious letters, reports to the board, orphanage history, and forged college and medical school records. In so doing he creates Dr. F. Stone, dedicated missionary to the Third World, skilled pediatrician, antiabortionist, willing replacement for the aged-ageless Dr. Larch. Delighted with what he has wrought—"what a good story! thought Wilbur Larch" (260)—he had only to wait until this intricate fiction would become reality. When Homer is finally ready to accept the fact that he "belonged to St. Cloud's," his death and re-creation as a fully detailed persona await only his free acceptance of Larch's creation.

"Playing God"

Irving's use of Larch as surrogate artist in *Cider House* is little more than a reflex action, however, and it is actually subsumed by a larger trope. It is significant that Homer, not Larch, is most deeply implicated in the novel's theme of rules and the tensions they produce— Larch orders his own world. While he recognizes the incongruities between personal desires and public discipline, he yet "knew what he was doing." It is true that, like Homer, he had felt guilt early; Larch had slept with a prostitute (later to die in his care) and refused the woman's daughter an abortion. But once the logic of his life is established—he would deliver babies *and* mothers—he would concern himself only with means, not ends.

Out of the natural chaos (unhumanized landscape, lowering clouds, hostile climate) and the human disorder (crumbling buildings and human flotsam of an abandoned lumber town), Larch creates the St. Cloud's orphanage. He actually wills it into existence for, though his nickname will be St. Larch, he is really a god. St. Cloud's is both pre– and postlapsarian; in Homer, Irving has created an innocent Adam who will be seduced by Melony, a perverse and violent Eve (later to pursue him through the apple orchards of Maine). But St. Cloud's is also a fallen place, the world as we know it. Larch's work there results both from individual and collective human failure (a work first demanded, ironically, by prostitutes), and from the outset he "undertook the task of righting the wrongs of St. Cloud's . . . a place where evil has so clearly flourished" (20), a place abandoned by the Ramses Paper Company, whose name combines a sly reference to popular contraceptives with a reference to the exploitive capitalistic pharaohs of the world.

It is clear that, however much Irving considers *Cider House* as history and polemic, the novel's mode (as we have seen the case to be with *Hotel New Hampshire*) is deeply influenced by romance. Against a background of realistic detail and in the context of American history, Irving places the character (caricature?) of Dr. Larch, a figure that Doris Grumbach (perceptively recognizing the importance of romance in his fiction) calls "God the Father." For Grumbach, *Cider House* is one more of Irving's "pure, unadulterated fairy tales" for adults, a "mythical tale of good and evil," not a novel attempting social realism.[23] Surely Irving would agree.

Melony (as an evil Eve she is associated in Irving's fable with the snake and penis) accuses Dr. Larch of "playing God—he gives you your history, or he takes it away" (103); later, as we have seen, we discover this to be exactly the case. Homer thinks that "Dr. Larch played God pretty well" and Larch himself writes in his history: "Here in St. Cloud's . . . I have been given the choice of playing God or leaving practically everything up to chance" (103), another of Irving's allegorical jokes. Consequently, the rules are "*his* rules" and "the only law at St. Cloud's . . . was Larch's law" (101). Aloof, spartan, sexless (and surrounded by celibate nurses, one of whom is actually named Angela), rumored never to sleep, possessed of "certain remote habits and singular powers" (93), Larch "plays God" to the degree possible in a limited universe. And true to his counterpart in Milton's fable, Larch finally allows Homer the choice appropriate to man's free will, ready to place his faith in Homer's innate goodness rather than in his own absolute power.

The novel's mythic element is slightly diminished as we move with Homer from St. Cloud's (a place that, however grim, is so isolated as to seem otherworldly) to Ocean View on the more populous coast, but it by no means disappears. The Worthington farm is one more in a long list of Irving's idyllic New England retreats, and the shift there in the novel's action is heralded by the arrival at St. Cloud's of a golden Wally and Candy, an alternative Adam and Eve whose beauty is so overwhelming that everyone at the ugly orphanage instantly falls in love with them—even Larch. (Their appearance in the white Cadillac convertible reminds us of the man in the white dinner jacket whose arrival by white sloop at Arbuthnot-by-the-Sea in *Hotel New Hampshire* sets in motion Win Berry's fatal dreams; both the man and the young couple promise an escape that, if eventually proven impossible, is nonetheless vibrant with human desire.)

The life at Ocean View is impinged upon by personal failure, disease, disloyalty, social dissonance, war, and even murder, but it retains through it all the insulating power of the pastoral. The ubiquitous apple, however, continues the symbolic reference of St. Cloud's and suggests that where there is an Eden there is a Fall. But is there one here?

Beyond the Undertoad

Irving's virtue has always been energy and abundance as opposed to meticulous craftsmanship; local failures have never seemed to worry him or distract his readers. And in *Cider House*, too, there are a number of irritating minor lapses: personal ticks from previous books, occasionally labored prose or caseworker talk, little litanies repeated with maddening frequency ("in other parts of the world," "as they say in Maine," "wait and see"), kisses in embarrassing abundance, and pages drenched in superfluous tears. The deaths of several minor characters (especially Ray Kendall, Olive Worthington, and Grace Lynch) are obviously just acts of tidying up, not the products of fictional logic. There are several weak scenes (as in the death of Fuzzy Stone and Melony's confrontation with Homer) and two obligatory scenes are unaccountably missing (Homer's long-delayed explanation of Angel's parentage to the boy and Candy's similarly postponed confession to Wally). There are moments, too, when Bogus Trumper's narrative theory in *Water-Method Man* seems a little too close to Irving's own assumptions about the literature of mass appeal: "you should always tell stories . . . in such a way that you make the audience feel good and wise, even a little ahead of you" (340). That the baby Rose Rose carries is her father's, for instance, or that Homer will go back to St. Cloud's, are examples of Trumper's theory at work.

For the Dickensian novelist, however, these could remain acceptable flaws; far more important is what seems to be missing from the book. A consistent element in all of Irving's previous fiction has been a lurking violence, not as an exception to normal existence but as its hallmark: "When I write a novel [he has said], I believe that it's necessary to have as much damage in it as I can imagine. It's necessary to spill both as much blood as I can and to retrieve as many souls as I can."[24] Best symbolized by the ubiquitous "undertoad" in *Garp*, this constant presence of unpredictable danger has been a distinguishing feature of his fiction and the source of critical controversy. But even those appalled by his use of violence have recognized it as the source of great *energy* in his fiction; the vigorous polarity of his vision—love and violence—has been the powerful engine that drives his plots. These oppositions have produced the peculiarly Irvingesque comic-tragic vision and it, in turn, has been the source of his unique tone.

In *Cider House*, however, the "lunacy and sorrow" have been reduced to eccentricity and sadness. "Without contraries there is no progression," William Blake would say; if Larch is God the Father, nowhere in the novel can one find his cosmic opposition. The result is, for Irving's fiction, a strangely predictable world. Unpleasant, ugly, and cruel things still happen and unpleasant people (though far fewer) still exist. But the radical disorder, the "terrifying contingency," has been muted and an altogether cozier, less dangerous and fecund world has taken its place: Bruegel has become Norman Rockwell. Despite all the gruesomeness of the world of abortion—the red, winking eyes of infected wombs and the pallid corpses of underdeveloped fetuses—the "evils" of abortion somehow do not bring us face to face with the evil that is for Irving "the leer of the world." The undertoad has, at least for the moment, withdrawn, and with it has gone what Miller finds missing from Irving's early short stories, his "comic, baroque, exaggerated style."[25]

Afterword

John Irving, the author of six books, is a veteran of lean years as an aspiring novelist and rich years as a hugely popular author. He is, however, only forty-four years old and he has already demonstrated a considerable capacity for change: no one reading the acerbic *158-Pound Marriage* in 1974 would have been likely to predict the explosive comic-tragic novel *Garp* published only four years later. If we have spoken in the foregoing study as though the die were cast, it was not our intention; any judgment of a living author at Irving's stage of development must necessarily be very tentative.

The World According to Garp unquestionably remains—both aesthetically and in terms of comprehensive appeal—Irving's most successful novel. Some critics, who had admired his earlier books for more "sophisticated" elements, rejected this new, ambitious, expansive novel without actually examining it closely enough to realize that it combined many artistic elements from the earlier works with a new commitment to "accessibility." Intellectually and emotionally rich, complexly, yet lucidly structured and energetically written, it will remain, we believe, a major novel of the last years of this century. The succeeding *Hotel New Hampshire* and *Cider House Rules*, the first exploring further the possibilities of romance and the second moving forcefully into "polemic," possess *Garp*-like qualities as well, but clearly embody the peculiar elements of his best novel less successfully.

In our view, the question now is whether Irving will commit himself single-mindedly to "audience," (about which he increasingly speaks), or whether he will seek again the ambitious fusion of *Garp*. There are those, no doubt, who would question the feasibility of such a simultaneous dedication to the honesty of personal vision and broad appeal, yet *Garp* has demonstrated that such a dual motive need not lead to artistic schizophrenia. Irving's enormous success, moreover, now gives him the independence and audience that allow maximum artistic integrity. If he surrenders to popularity he will become merely one more major commercial success who has written one remarkable novel; if he maintains the integrity of his vision while at the same time continuing to take seriously the largest possible audience, he may repeat and even surpass that which he has so far achieved.

Notes and References

Preface

1. R. Z. Sheppard, *Time,* 31 August 1981, 51.
2. William H. Pritchard, "Novel Discomforts and Delights," *Hudson Review* 35 (Spring 1982):159.

Chapter One

1. *The Hotel New Hampshire* (first published in 1981), paperback edition (New York: Pocket Books, 1982). All subsequent references to and quotations from Irving's five other novels will be from the following editions: *Setting Free the Bears* (first published in 1968), (New York: Pocket Books, 1979); *The Water-Method Man* (first published in 1972), (New York: Pocket Books, 1978); *The 158-Pound Marriage* (first published in 1974), (New York: Pocket Books, 1978); *The World According to Garp* (first published in 1978), (New York: Pocket Books, 1979); *The Cider House Rules* (New York: William Morrow & Co., 1985). Page numbers appear in parentheses following the citation.
2. Sheppard, *Time,* 46–51. Sheppard does, however, go on to say several useful things about Irving's fiction and *The Hotel New Hampshire.*
3. *Mademoiselle,* February 1983, 202.
4. Ibid.
5. Ibid.
6. *Vogue,* April 1979, 156.
7. *Ms.,* July/August 1982, 102–4. The citation adds: "for writing about rape with its true terror and brutality; for creating male characters who care about kids; and for understanding that feminist excesses are funny" (104).
8. Marilyn French, "The 'Garp' Phenomenon," *Ms.,* September 1982, 14–16. Though Irving understandably resents this often wrong-headed article ("it was stupid"; see *Mademoiselle,* 158), it nevertheless contains some valuable observations on his work.
9. Sheppard, *Time,* 51.
10. *USA Today,* 23 May 1985, 1D.
11. Pocket Books edition, 1979. The movie version of *Garp* was a success; a film of *The Hotel New Hampshire* was a disaster.
12. We are indebted to the following sources for biographical information: Hugh M. Ruppersburg, "John Irving," in *Dictionary of Literary Biogra-*

phy: American Novelists Since World War II, vol. 6 (Detroit, Mich.: Bruccoli Clark Book, Gale Research Co., 1980), 153–61; Charles Moritz, ed., *Current Biography Yearbook 1979* (New York: H. W. Wilson Co., 1979), 178–81; R. Z. Sheppard; Gabriel Miller, *John Irving* (New York: Frederick Ungar, 1981), 1–8. (As the only full-length study of Irving to date, Miller's book contains helpful information and insightful analyses for which we are also grateful.)

13. Greil Marcus, "John Irving: The World of 'The World According to Garp,' " *Rolling Stone*, 13 December 1979, 71. (Interview.)

14. Sheppard, *Time*, 51.

15. Scot Haller, "John Irving's Bizarre World," *Saturday Review* 8, no. 9 (September 1981):34.

16. Ernest Hemingway, *Green Hills of Africa* (New York: Charles Scribner's Sons, 1935), 23. It is not surprising that mass media publications continually take note of Irving's considerable income and such recent acquisitions as a Massachusetts "ski house" and "beach cabin" on Long Island's expensive South Shore (e.g., *USA Today*, 23 May 1985, 2D).

17. *Vogue*, 156.

18. Ibid.

19. Larry McCaffery, "An Interview with John Irving," *Contemporary Literature* 23, no. 1 (Winter 1982):10–11.

20. Ibid., 11. Jane Bowers Hill's essay, "John Irving's Aesthetics of Accessibility," *South Carolina Review* 16, no. 1 (Fall 1983):38–44, offers a very useful discussion of this issue.

21. Interview, "Good Morning America," ABC, 10 September 1982.

22. Ibid.

23. Warren French, " 'The Death of the Hired Man': Modernism and Transcendence," in *Frost Centennial Essays III*, ed. Jac Tharpe, 392 (Jackson: University Press of Mississippi, 1978).

24. Interview with Laura de Coppet, *Book of the Month Club News*, November 1981, 5.

25. Interview, "Good Morning America," ABC, 10 September 1982.

26. De Coppet, *BMC News*, 5.

27. Marilyn French, " 'Garp' Phenomenon," 14.

28. Ruppersburg, "John Irving," 160.

29. As quoted by Eleanor B. Wymard from Irving's 1979 Mount Holyoke College reading. " 'A New Version of the Midas Touch': *Daniel Martin* and *The World According to Garp*," *Modern Fiction Studies* 27, no. 2 (Summer 1981):286.

30. Ibid.

31. John Gardner, *On Moral Fiction* (New York: Basic Books, 1978), 198.

Chapter Two

1. Miller, *Irving*, 46.
2. Cf. Siggy's "poem":
Fate waits.
While you hurry
Or while you wait,
It's all the same to Fate. (43)
3. French, " 'Garp' Phenomenon," 14.
4. For example, see 265, 280, 281, 284, 340.
5. Michael Priestley, "Structure in the Worlds of John Irving," *Critique: Studies in Modern Fiction* 23, no. 1, (1981):83.

Chapter Three

1. Marcus, "Irving" (interview), 72.
2. John Fowles, *Daniel Martin* (Boston: Little Brown, 1977), 402–3, 405.
3. Wymard, *"Daniel Martin* and *The World According to Garp,"* 284.
4. Interview, "Good Morning America," ABC, 10 September 1982.
5. Ruppersburg, "John Irving," 157.
6. Susanne K. Langer, *Feeling and Form* (New York: Charles Scribner's Sons, 1953), 328.
7. Northrop Frye, "The Argument of Comedy," in *English Institute Essays, 1948*, ed. D. A. Robertson, Jr., 60–61 (New York: Columbia University Press, 1949).
8. Helen Gardner, "As You Like It," in *More Talking of Shakespeare*, ed. John Garrett, (London: Theatre Arts Books, 1959), 21.
9. Miller, *Irving*, 58.

Chapter Four

1. Marcus, "Irving" (interview), 72.
2. Ibid.
3. Miller, *Irving*, 189.
4. Ibid., 83.
5. In "Novel Sex and Violence," *Hudson Review* 28 (Spring, 1975), William Pritchard argues that Irving is "very good at creating a human voice" and that the narrator "uses words well" (148–49). Pritchard seems not to have noticed how imprecisely the narrator uses words, a reflection of his ultimately incomplete understanding of the experience he attempts to re-create here.
6. Irving L. Zupnick, *Bruegel* (New York: McGraw Hill, 1970), 38.
7. Miller, *Irving*, 77.

8. In "Lovers and Losers," *New Leader*, 25 November 1974, 14, Pearl K. Bell accurately assesses the lack of artistic resolution in the novel: "along the way he has lost control of the affirmations his story is presumably meant to offer. Swathed in a tangle of irresolute hints and guesses, neither the wrestling nor the sex bestows sufficient substance or meaning to *The 158-Pound Marriage*, and one is left with a mood of shambling inconsequence."

Chapter Five

1. *The World According to Garp*, see discussion between Garp and Helen on "true" versus "what *really* happened," 271.

2. Miller, *Irving*, 207.

3. Ibid., 202.

4. Irving describes the inherent differences between the first and second parts of the novel: "I wanted to create characters whom I greatly admired and then bless them with incredibly good fortune in the first half of the novel. . . . Everything these people want they get, for a while. But in the second half of the novel, I visit all the worst kinds of extreme things on these people to see how they would deal with extremes of adversity, just as earlier they had to cope with success." McCaffery, "Interview with Irving," 15.

5. Sheppard, quoting a postcard to Irving's editor, Henry Robbins, *Time*, 51.

6. Priestley, "Structure," 95.

7. Ibid., 93.

8. In "Why Is John Irving So Popular?" *Commentary* 73, no. 6 (June 1982): 59–63, Joseph Epstein recognizes the importance of Helen's academic interests in relation to Irving's narrative experiments: "Garp's wife is a university teacher, who teaches among other things a course in narrative technique, but it is Irving who attempts to show how much technique a narrative can have" (62). To our knowledge, no one else has made this connection.

9. McCaffery, "Interview with Irving," 1.

10. Hill, "Irving's Aesthetics of Accessibility," 42.

11. Ibid., 41.

12. Ruppersburg, "John Irving," 160.

13. Priestley, "Structure," 96.

14. John Barth, *Letters* (New York: Putnam, 1979), 760.

15. Frederick R. Karl, *American Fictions 1940–1980* (New York: Harper Colophon Books, 1983), footnote, xii.

16. Miller, *Irving*, 110–11.

17. It is interesting that even in "Vigilance" the "I" narrator virtually assumes the role of a policeman: " 'This is a citizen arrest,' I said" (329). In this case, however, the failure of the story can be partially explained because

Garp and the ersatz policeman are clearly one and the same—no objective distance is actually created at all.

18. McCaffery, "Interview with Irving," 13.

19. Miller, *Irving*, 108–9.

20. In a recent interview with Esther B. Fein, *New York Times Book Review*, 26 May 1985, Irving admits that "in all my books, every act of sexual pleasure is extremely costly. It is part of the New England notion that for every pleasure taken, you must make amends" (25). So however much sex is an "act of terrific optimism," it also (and often ironically) exacts a heavy price.

21. Discussing Irving's interest in language, Larry McCaffery ("Interview with Irving," 16-17) has a revealing exchange with the novelist about this sequence in *Garp*.

McCAFFERY: In *Garp* you create several people with speech impediments—Tinch, Fletcher, the Ellen Jamesians; during his recovery period Garp even finds himself trapped in almost a parody of a communication dilemma. Obviously you share with many other contemporary writers a particular interest in this issue of communicating effectively through language, through symbols.

IRVING: Yes, I've been very conscious in my fiction of dealing with this idea of how difficult it is to express oneself, how precarious our hold on symbols is. In *Garp* I created that recovery scene to push this idea to a kind of extreme: here we have the writer, who deals with language in order to express himself, placed in a situation in which he can't make himself understood because the words he has at his disposal, on these slips of paper, are ludicrously inadequate to communicate his feelings. This is a problem we all face but with writers the situation is magnified.

22. McCaffery, "Interview with Irving," 10.

Chapter Six

1. Miller, *Irving*, 193.

2. In his analysis of *The Hotel New Hampshire*, Miller makes extensive references to Bruno Bettelheim, *The Uses of Enchantment* (New York: Vintage, 1977).

3. Richard Chase, *The American Novel and Its Tradition* (New York: Doubleday/Anchor, 1957), viii–ix.

4. Ibid., 243.

5. De Coppet, *BMC News*, 5.

6. Joseph Campbell, *The Hero with a Thousand Faces* (1949, reprint, Princeton, 1973), 30.

7. Miller, *Irving*, 138–39.

8. Robert Ornstein, "Fitzgerald's Fable of East and West," *College English* 23 (December 1956):141.

9. David L. Minter, "Dream, Design and Interpretation in *The Great Gatsby*," in *Twentieth Century Interpretations of "The Great Gatsby,"* ed. Ernest Lockridge, 89 (New Jersey: Prentice-Hall, 1968).

10. F. Scott Fitzgerald, *The Great Gatsby* (New York: Charles Scribner's Sons, 1925), 182. Subsequent page references appear in the text.

11. Edwin S. Fussell, "Fitzgerald's Brave New World," *Journal of English Literary History* 19 (December 1951):291.

12. Miller, *Irving*, 193.

13. Interview, "Good Morning America," ABC, 10 September 1982.

14. Nathaniel Hawthorne, "The Custom House," in *The Scarlet Letter* (New York: W. W. Norton and Co., 1961 critical edition), 31.

15. Chase, *American Novel*, 7–8.

16. Ibid., 2.

17. Ibid., 1.

18. Ibid., xii.

Chapter Seven

1. McCaffery, "Interview with Irving," 10.

2. *USA Today*, 2D.

3. Ibid., 1D.

4. McCaffery, "Interview with Irving," 11.

5. Walter Clemons, "Dr. Larch's Odd Orphanage," *Newsweek*, 27 May 1985, 80.

6. McCaffery, "Interview with Irving," 12.

7. Benjamin DeMott, "Guilt and Compassion," *New York Times Book Review*, 26 May 1985, 25.

8. McCaffery, "Interview with Irving," 8.

9. *New York Times Book Review*, 25 November 1979, 3.

10. McCaffery, "Interview with Irving," 8. Like Dickens, however, his characters can sometimes take on a cartoonlike element. This is especially true of his minor characters, but in *Cider House* even Homer and Dr. Larch have something of this quality.

11. Hill, "Irving's Aesthetics of Accessibility," 39.

12. McCaffery, "Interview with Irving," 10.

13. *USA Today*, 1D–2D.

14. McCaffery, "Interview with Irving," 9, 10.

15. Interview, "All Things Considered," National Public Radio, 22 May 1985; *Book of the Month Club News*, Summer 1985, 5.

16. Ibid. Irving's father, flying with the army air force, was shot down

over Burma in World War II. Though he survived the war, Irving has no idea of his subsequent fate.

17. Fein, *New York Times Book Review* interview, 25.
18. DeMott, "Guilt and Compassion," 1.
19. National Public Radio interview.
20. DeMott, "Guilt and Compassion," 25.
21. Ibid. DeMott opens the second to last paragraph of his long review with: "viewed in literary terms, 'The Cider House Rules' is hardly without defect," reserving for this one short, late paragraph critical issues that should inform the whole of his essay. Such subordination of aesthetics to ideology illustrates an understandable but nonetheless unfortunate willingness to cheer on a humanistic warrior and ignore the artistic losses.
22. National Public Radio interview.
23. Morning Edition, National Public Radio, 23 May 1985.
24. *Record* (New Jersey), 25 March 1983, A21.
25. Miller, *Irving*, 5.

Selected Bibliography

PRIMARY SOURCES

1. Novels
Setting Free the Bears. New York: Random House, 1968. Reprint. New York: Pocket Books, 1979
The Water-Method Man. New York: Random House, 1972. Reprint. New York: Pocket Books, 1978
The 158-Pound Marriage. New York: Random House, 1974. Reprint. New York: Pocket Books, 1978
The World According to Garp. New York: E. P. Dutton, 1978. Reprint. New York: Pocket Books, 1979
The Hotel New Hampshire. New York: E. P. Dutton, 1981. Reprint. New York: Pocket Books, 1982
The Cider House Rules. New York: William Morrow, 1985.

2. Selected Edition
Three by Irving. New York: Random House, 1980. (*Setting Free the Bears, The Water-Method Man, The 158-Pound Marriage*, introduced by Terence DesPres.)

3. Short Stories (excluding those subsequently included in the novels) and selected essays arranged chronologically
"A Winter Branch." *Redbook*, November 1965, 56, 143–46.
"Weary Kingdom." *Boston Review*, Spring-Summer 1968, 8–35.
"Lost in New York." *Esquire*, March 1973, 117, 152.
"Almost in Iowa." *Esquire*, November 1973, 144–46, 224–29.
"Brennbar's Rant." *Playboy*, December 1974, 137, 304–7.
"Students: These Are Your Teachers!" *Esquire*, September 1975, 68, 156–59.
"Best Seller: What Does It Really Mean?" *Vogue*, April 1979, 154, 156.
"Kurt Vonnegut and His Critics." *New Republic*, 22 September 1979, 41–49.
"In Defense of Sentimentality." *New York Times Book Review*, 25 November 1979, 3, 96.
"Interior Space." *Fiction* 6 (1980); 26–58. (Written in 1974.)

SECONDARY SOURCES

1. Book
Miller, Gabriel. *John Irving*. New York: Frederick Ungar Publishing Co., 1982. A thorough and interesting interpretive study through *The Hotel New Hampshire*. Includes select biographical and bibliographical information and an interview with Irving.

2. Parts of Books, Articles, and Selected Reviews
Atlas, James. "John Irving's World." *New York Times Book Review*, 13 September 1981, 1, 36, 38, 40. Harsh review of *Hotel New Hampshire* which, however, fairly delineates Irving's strengths and shortcomings.
Bell, Pearl K. "Lovers and Losers." *New Leader*, 25 November 1974, 13–14. One of the rare discussions of *Marriage*; a balanced evaluation.
Chase, Richard. *The American Novel and Its Tradition*. New York: Doubleday/Anchor, 1957. Seminal and continuously useful discussion of the American novel as romance, particularly as it illuminates Irving's last two novels.
Clemons, Walter. "Dr. Larch's Odd Orphanage." *Newsweek*, 27 May 1985, 80. Hostile but insightful review of *Cider House*.
De Coppet, Laura. *Book of the Month Club News*, November 1981, 4–5. Irving discusses *Hotel New Hampshire*.
DeMott, Benjamin. "Domesticated Madness." *Atlantic Monthly* 248, no. 4 (October 1981): 101–2, 104–6. See annotation below.
————."Guilt and Compassion." *New York Times Book Review*, 26 May 1985, 1, 25. Like its predecessor review on *Hotel*, a thoughtful, persuasive analysis of *Cider House* which argues strongly on Irving's behalf, but does so primarily for humanistic, rather than aesthetic, reasons.
Drabble, Margaret. "Muck, Memory, and Imagination." *Harper's*, July 1978, 82–84. Interesting analysis of *Garp* which focuses on aesthetic themes.
Epstein, Joseph. "Why Is John Irving So Popular?" *Commentary* 73, no. 6 (June 1982): 59–63. Irving as popular novelist.
Fein, Esther. "Costly Pleasures." *New York Times Book Review*, 26 May 1985, 25. Comments by Irving on *Cider House*.
French, Marilyn. "The 'Garp' Phenomenon." *Ms.*, September 1982, 14–16. Penetrating feminist discussion of *Garp* and film of same.
Gray, Paul. "An Orphan or an Abortion." *Time*, 3 June 1985, 81. A sympathetic review of *Cider House*.
Haller, Scot. "John Irving's Bizarre World." *Saturday Review* 8, no. 9 (September 1981): 30–32, 34. Insights into Irving's milieu; biographical information, and commentary from Irving.

Hill, Jane Bowers. "John Irving's Aesthetics of Accessibility: Setting Free the Novel." *South Carolina Review* 16, no. 1 (Fall 1983): 38–44. Admiring and perceptive study of Irving's aesthetics.

Karl, Frederick R. *American Fictions 1940–1980.* New York: Harper Colophon Books, 1983. Views Irving as generally inferior to more academically oriented contemporary figures.

Lounsberry, Barbara. "The Terrible Under Toad: Violence as Excessive Imagination in *The World According to Garp.*" *Thalia* 5, no. 2 (Fall/Winter 1982–83): 30–35. Interesting, if moralistic, treatment of extremism in *Garp.*

Lyons, Gene. "Something New in Theme Parks." *Nation* 233, no. 9 (26 September 1981): 101–2, 104–6. Caustic review of *Hotel* combined with praise for Irving's past achievements and potential.

Marcus, Greil. *Rolling Stone,* 27 June 1978, 24 August 1978, 21 September 1978. Various admiring and perceptive pieces on Irving with particular attention to *Garp.*

———. "John Irving: The World of *The World According to Garp.*" *Rolling Stone,* 13 December 1979, 68–75. Excellent, often quoted, interview.

McCaffery, Larry. "An Interview with John Irving." *Contemporary Literature* 23, no. 1 (Winter 1982): 1–18. Seminal interview.

Moritz, Charles, ed. *Current Biography Yearbook 1979,* 178–81. New York: H. W. Wilson Co., 1979. Useful biographical data.

Nelson, William. "Unlikely Heroes: The Central Figures in *The World According to Garp, Even Cowgirls Get the Blues,* and *A Confederacy of Dunces.*" In *The Hero in Transition.* Edited by Ray B. Brown, 163–70. Bowling Green: Bowling Green University Popular Press, 1983. Discussion of bizarre heroes and the comic-grotesque mode.

Priestley, Michael. "An Interview with John Irving." *New England Review,* Summer 1979, 489–504. Interesting and revealing early interview.

———. "Structure in the Worlds of John Irving." *Critique: Studies in Modern Fiction* 23, no. 1 (1981): 82–96. One of the most serious and penetrating of analyses; focuses on juxtaposition of aesthetic/humanistic issues.

Pritchard, William H. "Novel Sex and Violence." *Hudson Review* 28 (Spring 1975): 147–60. A positive analysis of *Marriage* within the context of novels published contemporaneously.

———. "Novel Discomforts and Delights." *Hudson Review* 35 (Spring 1982): 159–76. A harsh analysis of *Hotel* within the context of novels published contemporaneously.

Reilly, Edward C. "The *Anschluss* and the World According to Irving." *Research Studies* 51, no. 2 (June 1983): 98–110. Excellent background material on Irving's *Anschluss* metaphor.

Ruppersburg, Hugh M. "John Irving." In *Dictionary of Literary Biography: American Novelists Since World War II.* Vol. 6, 153. Detroit: Gale Research Co. Useful, comprehensive sketch of writer and career; critical analysis relatively limited.

Sheppard, R. Z. "Life into Art." *Time*, 31 August 1981, 18–28. Cover story and sympathetic career assessment through *Hotel*; useful details.

Story, Richard David. "Wild Novels, Extravagant Success." *USA Today*, 23 May 1985, 1–2D. Statements by and about Irving and his "success" on the publication of *Cider House*.

Suplee, Curt. "John Irving and the Tyranny of Imagination." *Washington Post*, 25 August 1981, B1, B8–9. An informal mixture of quotes from an interview, biographical information, and limited analyses of *Garp* and *Hotel*.

Sweet, Ellen. "Men Who've Taken Chances and Made a Difference." *Ms.*, July/August 1982, 102–4. Irving as popular—and feminist—hero.

Thompson, Christine E. "Pentheus in *The World According to Garp*." *Classical and Modern Literature* 3, no. 1 (Fall 1982): 33–37. Pentheus myth used to illuminate "First Feminist Funeral" sequence in *Garp*.

Tyler, Anne. "Three by Irving." *New Republic* 128, no. 17 (26 April 1980). Intelligent and sympathetic analysis (by a self-described *Garp*-hater and novelist) of Irving's first three novels with particular praise for *Water-Method Man*.

"Women According to John Irving." *Mademoiselle*, February 1983, 158, 202. Sympathetic synopsis of interview.

Wymard, Eleanor B. "A New Version of the Midas Touch: *Daniel Martin* and *The World According to Garp*." *Modern Fiction Studies* 27, no. 2 (Summer 1981): 284–86. An insightful comparison of the two novels—and writers—in relation to postmodernism.

Index